NOT WANTED

DAYTON LUMMIS

iUniverse, Inc.
New York   Bloomington

Not Wanted

iUniverse books may be ordered through booksellers or by contacting:

iUniverse
1663 Liberty Drive
Bloomington, IN 47403
www.iuniverse.com
1-800-Authors (1-800-288-4677)

ISBN: 978-1-4401-7971-6 (sc)
ISBN: 978-1-4401-7972-3 (ebk)

Printed in the United States of America

iUniverse rev. date: 10/07/2009

Dedicated to the Memory of the Bishop Family:

Lobelia Bishop
Annette Bishop
William Bradford Bishop, III
Brenton Bishop
Geoffery Bishop

Contents

INTRODUCTION

In the Class Book for the 50th Reunion of the Class of 1959 of Yale University there is an entry for every member of the class. Some are rather long autobiographical pieces, others rather brief and to the point, just names, photos and addresses. Under the name William Bradford Bishop, Jr., there is no photo, only a very brief entry:

"Address Unavailable."

That must be one of the great understatements of all time!

I.

WHERE TO BEGIN?

I begin where I begin…

In June of 1972 I assumed the position of Director of the Cripple Creek District Museum in the old mining town of Cripple Creek, 9500' high on the west slope of Pike's Peak in Colorado. The museum was open seven days a week from May through October, but in the winter months it was open only on weekends, and then often with only very few visitors. I spent the first lonely winter in Cripple Creek because I thought it was my job and the challenge was interesting. I spent the second winter because I thought I had better, to show that "I could take it." And I spent the third winter realizing that in reality I did not have to be there all winter, that the old ladies were perfectly capable of running the place for a few months. So, during the winter of 1975-76 I took a few months away from Cripple Creek, and after Christmas with my father in Santa Monica, California, moved up to Berkeley and occupied the basement apartment of Ted and Janet Woodhams-Roberts' house. Ted was an old friend who had "hired" me, on rather generous terms, to assist in the renovation of his Berkeley Hills house.

That was what I was doing in March of 1976, when my father came up from Santa Monica for a visit. He stayed in the comfortable Hotel Berkeley, and I would go down to join him for breakfast. Which is what I did on the morning of 9 March 1976. My father was seated at his customary table, with a croissant and a cup of coffee. He was reading, as he did when in San Francisco, an edition of *The Chronicle*. He looked up as I approached and sat down. I thought that, for some reason, he looked rather grim. He handed me the paper, pointing to a news item in the lower right hand column. I was shocked and dismayed as I read:

"5 IN MD. FAMILY FOUND SLAIN
Killed in Home, Dumped in N.C.; Father Missing

Five members of a Bethesda family—the wife, mother and three sons of a missing State Department official—were beaten to death in their house last week and then driven to North Carolina, where their bodies were set afire in an open grave.

The victims were identified yesterday as members of the Bradford Bishop family of 8103 Lilly Stone Dr., Carderock Springs. Police said the pajama-clad bodies of William Bradford III, 14; Brenton G., 10, and Geoffery, 6, were found in the fiery grave beneath their fully clothed mother, Annette, 37, and paternal grandmother, Lobelia Bishop, 68.

Montgomery County police said last night that bloodstains were found in all four bedrooms of the Bishop's $100,000 contemporary split-level home. Other bloodstains were found in the driveway, they said.

Col. Phillip Caswell, the police spokesman, said police found no weapon and there was "no struggle in the house as far as we can tell."

He said police believe the killings occurred about 6:30 p.m. on Monday, March 1, and that the bodies were carried out the front door. The Bishops' station wagon was seen near the gravesite, in desolate Tyrell County, N.C., about 10 a.m. the next morning. About three hours later a forest ranger spotted a fire that turned out to be the burning grave.

The Yale educated Bishop, 39, is assistant chief of the special trade activities office of the State Department's economic and business section.

He was listed by Montgomery County police last night as a "missing person" and police public information officer Dick Green said Bishop is being sought for questioning…"

I read the article twice, not quite believing what I was reading. Shock and a terrible sadness. But something else, something strange that I repressed, mostly. It was a slight ember of thought that I somehow knew Brad Bishop might be capable of something like this, horrible and hard to understand as it might be. He had been my only roommate senior year in Calhoun College at Yale University. Was there something about my old college roommate that I had glimpsed and then banished from my mind? Some curious, twisted, suppressed rage against the world? A desire for some form of "revenge"? Some long smoldering emotions that suddenly burst forth to cause this brutal and unspeakable crime? I remembered reading a disturbing comment by Goethe: "There is no crime so horrible that I do not feel myself in some way capable of committing." Was Bishop's crime something lurking in the psyche of all of us?

I put the paper down and looked at my father, who shook his head gravely. During breakfast we discussed what had allegedly happened, expressing disbelief and great sadness. Then we spent the rest of the day around Berkeley and Oakland, not discussing the Bishop matter, but it was locked in our thoughts. How could it not be?

My father and I had an early supper and I repaired to the Roberts home in the Berkeley Hills. Ted and Janet had just finished dinner, and both had read *The Chronicle* that morning. Of course they had noticed the front page article about a Yale graduate who had evidently murdered his entire family and was a fugitive. Noting the man's age, 39, same as mine, they wondered if I had known the fellow? Known! I snorted—"He was my roommate senior year." "How awful," Janet murmured, and Ted just shook his head. I asked if I could use the phone downstairs to call Lionel Alves (known in college as "Dr. Avis, and henceforth will be so referred to as) in Greeley, Colorado, where he taught history at Northern Colorado University. The Doctor had been part of our "group" at Yale, and had, as had I, last seen Bishop in San Francisco in the winter of 1964. They had both been in the Army Language School at Monterey, California, and had gone on to serve in the Army Security Agency, listening to Eastern Block military radio traffic in Europe. Ted said, "Sure, go ahead," so I went downstairs and placed the call to Greeley. The Doctor picked right up, and said he had been waiting for my call. He had seen the news article, also a TV segment, and wanted to talk about Bishop and "the tragedy."

After some discussion about how could such a horrible thing happen, what drives a person to do something like that, we talked about Bishop's visit to San Francisco just before Christmas in 1964. I reminded the Doctor that I had seen Brad shortly before that, over Thanksgiving in Southern California.

Meredith had come down to spend Thanksgiving with me and my father. A note arrived from Bishop, whom I had not seen since the Yale graduation in June of 1959, asking if I might be visiting my father over Thanksgiving, and if so, why not come over to his parents' house in South Pasadena for a visit? He enclosed the telephone number. I got him on the line and arranged for me and Meredith to visit on Saturday afternoon.

It was one of those remarkably clear days in Los Angeles, occurring recently less and less, when the snowcapped mountains behind Pasadena were sparkling clear. We turned off the Arroyo Seco Freeway into South Pasadena—which most decidedly is not elegant and wealthy Pasadena, but rather a solid middle class Southern California Anglo community. The Bishop house we found easily, on a tree shaded quiet side street. It was the house that Brad had grown up with, as an only child. We were welcomed warmly by Brad and his wife Annette. Inside Brad's father—a sort of "Okie good ole boy," in spite of his lineage, was watching a football game. I knew he was an oil leaser up around Bakersfield in Kern County, where his type was legion. About all he had to say as we settled into the living room was, "Y'all want a beer? Get some outta the fridge." Brad's mother was charming if a bit intense. I could tell that it had been her influence that had pushed Brad toward Yale. She chatted with us briefly, then excused herself saying that she "had things to do." I remembered the parents and Annette from the Yale graduation, but not well. We did not stay long. Meredith chatted with Annette while Brad told me that he had studied the Serbo-Croatian language further after taking it at Monterey. He told me that he had finished an intensive course in Italy at the University of Padua, and the Army had sent him to UCLA for a semester of study of Balkan history and culture. It sounded rather interesting, but suddenly Brad had nothing more to say on the subject. We talked of Dr. Avis who had established himself in San Francisco. Brad mentioned that he and Annette would be in San Francisco for a few days just before Christmas, that we should all get together for dinner. I agreed, and noticed that Meredith was signaling that we should go. We took our leave of that bright and chintzy, very bland and middle class living room. Brad's father waved a beer can at us as we left. His mother did not seem to be around.

After reminding the Doctor of that visit, we talked of the get-together in San Francisco. The Doctor remembered a rather boring evening. He recalled that when he and Brad had been at the Army Language Institute, Brad had hung around with a rather "elite" bunch of guys, who acted as if they were something special, and that he had not had much to do with the Doctor. So much for the old college friendship. I think that affected the Doctor's mood at dinner. He did remember a few things. One was how Brad has expressed envy at the sort of free-spirited life that we were living in San Francisco, that he had gotten himself tied up in things somewhat beyond his control, that he was committed to. He did not get specific, and it seemed a bit convoluted for the role of an enlisted man in the Army. He spoke about Italy, nothing about Yugoslavia and the Doctor assumed that his Serbo-Croatian studies were to further enable him to evaluate military and radio communications emanating from that country. I wondered what a semester of study of Balkan history and culture might have to do with that, but the question never came up. After we dropped the Doctor off we joined Brad and Annette at a rather imposing house in Pacific Heights where they said they were guests—of whom it was never said. I thought there was something a bit off about the arrangement, and so did Meredith—as if that large house with seemingly no other residents was some sort of "CIA House" or something. Vivid imagination!

That is the gist of what the Doctor and I talked about that night—the last time we had seen Brad. The Doctor did mention that when he was teaching in Uganda, Africa, in the 1970s he heard that Brad was with the State Department assigned to a diplomatic post in Botswana, under an Ambassador Korry. It was said, in gossip among Americans living and working in Africa, that the Ambassador called Bishop "My fair-haired boy." The Doctor added another piece of gossip, that "Ambassador Korry is some sort of troubleshooter for the State Department, and everywhere he goes somebody dies." The Doctor said he had no idea whether there was any truth in that, it was just something that he had heard.

We talked over the next few months about the case, about various news items that appeared in the press about Bishop the fugitive. Then, with nothing happening, we talked less and less about the matter.

The next day my father returned to Santa Monica, and that evening I got a call from him saying that the FBI had contacted him wanting to know my whereabouts, saying that people in Cripple Creek did not know where I was. Assuring him that they only wanted to interview me about any possible clues, or thoughts, I might have as to where Bishop might have fled to. They were interviewing everyone he had ever known, they said. So, he gave them Ted's number in Berkeley.

The next morning an FBI agent called asking if they might have a few moments of my time in Berkeley later that morning. I agreed, giving them the address and directions. About 11 a.m. I was working in the front of the house when I saw what was obviously a government issue Crown Victoria park down below on Keith Avenue. And emerging from it two "from central casting" federal agents, one young and one older, in ties and sport coats.

I welcomed them to the living room and we all sat down. Ted and Janet were both out. The younger agent looked at me and said, smiling, "You look in good shape, you've lost a lost of weight." I must have looked surprised (to say the least) because they both chuckled. Then I remembered and said, "The background check in 1964?" They nodded. I had been working part-time at Reginald Jones Design Associates in downtown San Francisco when the FBI came calling. Seems my old classmate Bishop had applied for "a sensitive government position," and they had some routine background questions to ask. Did Bishop exhibit any homosexual tendencies? Did he drink excessively? Did he express sentiments against the government or establishment? Did he seem emotionally and psychologically stable? Things like that. I gave very positive answers and hoped that Brad got whatever job he was applying for. I had no idea what that might be. Evidently those agents had given a physical description of me at that time, noting that I was "overweight." Which I had been. These two agents in the living room in Berkeley had obviously read that previous report, and were now noticing that I had considerably slimmed down.

I told these fellows that I had not seen nor heard from Bishop since 1964, that I had no idea what he had been doing, and that the allegations of these crimes were a great shock to me. They said that they understood, but they wanted to go back to the college years. Had Brad ever talked about any mountain hideaways, places, say, in the Northwest that he had hiked or fished in, that he had been very fond of? Obviously they were grasping at straws. I told them that as far as I knew all Brad's outdoor experience had been in the mountains around LA. I had never heard him talk about any other parts of the country. What about Mexico? I did not recall Brad ever talking about Mexico. They thanked me and left. That was it...

Later that fall (1976) I took a short trip east after the museum closed weekdays for the winter. In New York I attended an event at The Yale Club, and there ran into a classmate who, I knew, had known Brad Bishop more than casually at Yale. We got to talking, naturally, about the case, how baffling, disturbing and tragic it was. My classmate mentioned that he too, in Washington, D.C., where he then lived, had an FBI visit. As with me, they were seeking leads, ideas, information as to where Bishop might have disappeared to and or might be hiding. And, as with me, he had nothing to offer except that Bishop had been stationed in the army in Italy. But they knew that. We talked about a news article that had appeared widely, giving details of Bishop's travel westward across North Carolina from the gravesite, where he stopped in a rural sporting goods store to use a credit card to make a purchase (reported at the time as a dog lead or leash, but later amended to other items.), and how Bishop's station wagon had been found abandoned in a parking lot on the FAR side of Great Smoky Mountains National Park, and how there had been no trace of Bishop anywhere since then. How did he get away? How odd?

My classmate mentioned that he and Brad were good friends during the time they had spent at the Monterey Language Institute. And that they had vacationed together on several occasions while he was in Germany and Brad in Italy in 1961-63. Then, he said, the trail goes cold—meaning that he and Brad were not in touch after that time. He also mentioned that Brad had been a sergeant in Army Intelligence and was planning to stay in the Army a bit longer than my classmate. Who was planning on discharge and law school. When I mentioned seeing Brad in South Pasadena over Thanksgiving in 1964, and how Brad had spoken of the Army sending him to UCLA for a semester studying Balkan history and culture, my classmate got interested. "Rather unusual," he said for a mere enlisted man. "I think they had something planned for Brad." Then he recalled: "On one of our visits, after a few drinks, Brad said that he was 'running some guy' in Yugoslavia, but nothing more." When I asked what he thought that meant, his answer was that he did not know. We left it at that—ancient history. We parted, promising to keep in touch.

A few weeks later, back in Colorado I sent him a short note, saying that I had been wondering about that "running some guy in Yugoslavia,"—was it in the government? That it seemed to me that was more something that an experienced CIA agent would do, not an enlisted man in Army Intelligence. Did he have anymore ideas on that?

A quick reply came back from my classmate: "Unlikely I got 'running some guy' from Brad, he was too discreet. It probably came from the FBI. Whatever the source, it seems he was 'running' a Yugo. From Brad I did know that he was on the 'offense' side, and was in touch with some Yugos, but no more details from him."

Well, from that it seemed to me that he was trying to distance himself from the "running" remark. Had it come from the FBI? Not likely. Even if they knew about that, why would they mention it in an interview that was to ostensibly learn if possible any hiding places, etc., that former friends and associates of Bishop might know about? No need to be bringing up long ago intrigue in Yugoslavia. Further, my classmate's affirmation that Brad was on the "offense" side and "was in touch with some Yugos," adding to "it seems he was running" a

Yugo, adds up to something more than just listening to military radio broadcasts out of Yugoslavia.

But none of that was anything to dwell on at the time, and the Bishop case sort of faded into the background for many years. Oh, there were some "sightings" that stirred the water, and some TV shows like *America's Most Wanted*, but generally no one had anything new to say. Bishop was gone, his family were all dead, and that was all there was to it…

II.

BISHOP AT YALE

I first met Brad Bishop in September of 1954. We were freshmen at Yale University, he by way of South Pasadena High School in Southern California, and I from The Haverford School, a boys' prep school on the Main Line outside of Philadelphia. Rather different backgrounds, one might say. Where we intersected at the beginning of that freshman year was in trying out for the freshman football team. We had, each of us, been better than average players on our respective teams, and thought it natural that we would continue our successes at Yale, beginning with the freshman team. We were both wrong.

We noticed very early on that the freshman team had already been chosen, from the star players that had been recruited by the coaches, many from Midwestern high schools. If any of the rest of us were to gain any attention it would have to be through very superior performance. Which we did not seem to be demonstrating. Further, it was obvious that the freshman team experience would be one of an exceeding "grind"—that is, football, study, and little if anything else. This was most emphatically demonstrated by two star freshman players across the hall from me at 197 Farnum. Winterbauer and Poindexter were both from suburban Chicago Catholic high schools. Winterbauer was a quarterback who could hit a dime throwing downfield, and Poindexter was a big, rangy end who could catch anything thrown near him. But, what impressed me was how focused and disciplined they were. Football practice all afternoon, into the evening hours. Dinner, study until 11 p.m., then to bed and up at 6 a.m. Day in and day out. I was not a freshman at Yale University to live that sort of existence.

Brad approached me on one of the first days of trying out for the freshman team. He said that he heard I was from California. Not really, I told him—I was in Santa Monica when I sent my picture in for the freshman handbook and that was the address they put down for me. If Brad was disappointed, he did not show it. He was very much a Southern California sort of guy—there was a sort of "stereotype" in those days. He had a rather unique way of talking, almost Midwestern, a slight Okie twang. Which I was later to learn came from his father. A few days later we got talking about football practice, how the team seemed to be already chosen, the total "grind" aspect of the experience—and we decided that we wanted more from our freshman experience at Yale. So, that was that…

For the rest of that freshman year I did not see much of Brad. We really did not seem to have all that much in common. I was surprised, however, to see that on the freshman campus he had sort of fallen in with a group of "preppies" from elite New England schools. Interesting, given Brad's sort of "Midwestern folksiness" and the aloof demeanor often typical of those preppies. And so it went.

Until in the late spring an "incident" befell me that made me a sort of minor celebrity in the freshman class. A group of us had been drinking beer at an establishment on Chapel Street called "The Silver Dollar." How that establishment got away with serving hordes of 18-year-old freshmen I do not know. I guess someone was paid off, big time. Anyway, toward closing time a few of our group got into a sort of scuffle out on the sidewalk with a couple of "townies"—i.e. locals who disliked and resented Yale students. Quite a few of us piled outside to see what was going on. And, simultaneously, several carloads of townies came cruising by, Seeing some of their brethren seemingly being set upon by a "mob" of Yalies, they leapt out of their cars armed with tire irons and chains. Quite a melee started. Several evidently had knives. I was more or less a by-stander to these events, but one of the townies backed me into a store doorway and took a wild swing at me. Oddly, he hit me in the thigh, but when he pulled his fist away I saw the glint of a small knife blade. Blood began to run down my leg. A classmate got me into a taxi and quickly to New Haven General Hospital. Where a few stitches were applied. The doctor told me I was lucky that the knife had not struck the big artery. If it had I might not have made it. Close call. But, luckily not a serious wound. A few other classmates were knocked around but not seriously injured. The incident was written up in both *The Yale Daily News* and the *New Haven Register*. Those of us who had sustained injuries were sorts of minor celebrities for a few weeks—the old fifteen minutes of fame syndrome. Brad and his prep school buddies sat down with me one evening in the freshman dining hall and wanted to hear all about the incident. I was tired of talking about it, but gave them a pretty good account. The preppies were not impressed with brawling in the streets of New Haven, but I think that perhaps Brad was—just a little bit. But, freshman year was nearly over and we were being assigned to the Yale colleges where we would spend the next three years. I say assigned because previous to that year colleges were acquired "by choice." The administration had decided that the colleges had become entirely too segregated by personalities and social standing, so it was decided to achieve more "diversity" through an impartial system of assignment. Brad and I were assigned to Calhoun College, which had a reputation of housing the "jocks" on campus. Most of the Haverford contingent at Yale ended up at Calhoun, as did my freshman roommate Chris Carroll, and Farnum entryway classmate Charles Constantin, from Dallas. Paul Hoffman, a Haverford grad, was relegated to Silliman College, which he hated because of it's reputation for being "for nerds"—i.e. engineering students. Hoffman had very definite social pretensions, and Silliman College did not suit those.

Sophomore year at Calhoun—in the fall, it was back to football. Yale had a very well developed intramural football program among the eight undergraduate colleges. Brad and I decided to give the Calhoun team a try, as did my roommate Charles Constantin. Practice was a couple of afternoons a week, for an hour or so. There was a "coach"; usually another classmate who had some football background. We suited up and played regular football games against the other colleges on Friday afternoons. It was informal and fun. Our Calhoun team was quite good. The players had all been better than average high school football players. We beat all the other colleges and won the intramural championship—for which we were awarded handsome medals. Then, on the weekend of the Yale-Harvard weekend, we played the champion of the Harvard intramural program. That year the games were in New Haven, and on a fine fall Friday afternoon we soundly defeated the Harvard chaps. (As did the undefeated Varsity team, with Winterbauer and Poindexter seeing quite a bit of playing time.) We gained another handsome medal and some mild notoriety. I remember that Brad was a great asset to our team. I could tell that he had been quite good back there at South Pasadena High School. Once he remarked that he might have been playing for Pasadena Junior College, in the warmth and sunshine, with a lot of pretty girls watching. Well, New Haven was sort of cool and gray, and monastic. Where were the pretty girls? After the games we would head to George & Harry's or The Old Heidelberg to celebrate. Quite a bit of beer went down. There was no talk about having to be "in shape."

After the football season I did not see much of Brad, just sat with him at dinner now and then when he was not with his preppie roommates, who seemed rather snobbish. I heard that Brad had pledged at the DKE fraternity, as had Charles Constantin. That was a fun loving bunch. The preppies gravitated to Fence Club; which had a very "social" reputation.

I grew increasingly ill at ease during my sophomore year, wondering what I was doing at Yale and what should I do with my life? Nothing seemed to come into focus. I neglected my studies and was well into the bottom half of my class. It did not seem to matter. In fact, at times nothing seemed to matter. I thought more and more about taking a year off "to think about things." In discussions with Dean Harold Whiteman, a most understanding man, I diplomatically referred to "a need to mature," to develop some aim and purpose in life. He agreed that a year off might be good, and that I would be guaranteed re-entry to Yale the following year. Paul Hoffman also left Yale, rather abruptly, under a cloud, during the spring of sophomore year. It seems there was "an incident" at the Stage Door Grill, near the Taft Hotel, and Hoffman had punched a bartender, shattering his cheekbone and knocking him through a window. Charges were brought, then "dealt with." But Hoffman was required to leave Yale, rather in disgrace, unsure if he would be allowed back. He was to spend a number of years in the Navy before he returned, a junior when I was a senior, after my year off. Brad Bishop, on the other hand, seemed popular, focused, and very definitely staying out of any sort of trouble.

I traveled to Mexico that summer, 1956, worked as a waiter at a posh Lake Tahoe resort into October, then returned to Philadelphia to wangle my way into some sort of maritime job—to see the world! I ended up on a Cities Service super tanker plying a route between the northeast and the Texas oil ports. Not much of seeing the world, but remunerative. I returned to Yale as a junior in the fall of 1957, somewhat more mature and rather more experienced, but not much focused on a post graduate career. I did, however, apply myself to my studies and struggled into the top half of my class. I noticed right off that Brad Bishop was not with us in Calhoun that fall. Word was that he "had taken a year off" (that would have been his senior year) for financial reasons, someone thought. But that did not make sense, because Yale always came to the rescue of anyone with "financial problems," either with a loan or a student job. So, it seemed that there must have been some other reason for Brad's absence. I was never to learn what that was. In retrospect I wonder if it might have been "something psychological."

(If the reader thinks that I have gone on too much in these pages about myself and trivial matters, allow me to comment that I am "setting the stage" for the senior year in which Brad Bishop and I were Calhoun College roommates in a suite with a living room and fireplace, and two separate bedrooms.)

My junior year roommates, a bunch of Haverfordians with two others had occupied a large suite of rooms. But, they had all graduated with the Class of 1958. So, when returning that fall I had not designated a roommate but had allowed Calhoun College to choose one for me. It was Brad Bishop, who had returned from whatever he had been doing in California to take his senior year and earn his Yale diploma. This I learned as I was unpacking in the top floor suite to which I had been assigned. Brad came "bouncing in," all good cheer and breeziness. I surmised that we would get along fine. We were both history majors, had a few interests in common, and knew how to stay out of each other's way. Neither of us particularly knew any one of our senior classmates, not anything more than to nod at. There was one other senior who had been a member of the Class of 1958. That was Lionel Alves, who, it was said, the previous year had simply walked out of an exam and disappeared. He later surfaced in Fort Lauderdale working at "Porky's," a popular local restaurant. The "walking out of an exam" part of the tale turned out to be not exactly true, as I learned talking with Lionel at the traditional fall introductory "get-together" called, interestingly enough, "Trolley Night." Lionel was a great Anglophile with a fascination with and encyclopedic knowledge of the British titled class. Plus an equally vast store of European history. His memory and recall were outstanding. One did not have to read the *New York Times* since Lionel could recapitulate virtually everything of importance in each issue—which he would regularly do over dinner. Brad found Lionel a bit odd, I think. Far removed from the "regular guy" sorts that he was used to. But, at the same time he was fascinated. As he was by some other strange types that Paul Hoffman, then returned to Silliman College as a junior, had gathered up. Like Winthrop Brainerd, the self-proclaimed "Arch Duke of Atrenia." Brad, who was smart and affable, was not particularly sophisticated either socially or culturally, and had not been around types like these. It was, I think, something of "a new world" for him. One that he seemed to observe rather than fully participate in. I think he was more comfortable with me, at George and Harry's talking over things Californian, with a few beers.

Nineteen fifty-eight was the period of the beatniks, whom we always sort of envied when we visited Greenwich Village, which we did from time to time. It was also the period when Jack Kerouac's smash novel, *On the Road*, hit the scene and awakened great wanderlust in American youth—along with a newly cultivated sense of irresponsibility. Brad and I spend a lot of time talking over these things, giving a lot of thought to "hitting the road" and just getting away from everything. We also devoted quite a bit of time to discussions on existentialism and nihilism, a large dose of which I was absorbing in Henri Peyre's fascinating course in "French Literature in Translation." Professor Peyre seemed to thrive on "being and nothingness," but the rest of us were somewhat disturbed. I remember Brad being rather upset at perhaps facing for the first time the notion that there is no purpose to life. That would throw him into one of the not infrequent depressions that he commented on. Not unusual—being "depressed" was mildly fashionable among students at that time. It was part of "growing up," or so it was thought. I remember on time Brad saying that he had been depressed, but one day he woke up and suddenly was "not depressed."

He wondered about that and commented, "And that really depressed me." An early awareness of one not being in control of one's mind and moods. As well as of "depression," which can grow into a debilitating syndrome. In all of our philosophic discussions we seemed to rather avoid much contemplation of the future. I never heard Brad discuss any possible career plans. We were more sunk into a sort of "here and now syndrome," contemplating existence as we found it. Not involved in any meaningful planning for the future. I think that was something we felt uncomfortable about. Brad did talk about his high school sweetheart, Annette, the cheerleader. Whether he should—or should have (leading me to wonder about that year off and what he did back in Southern California?) married her. He often meandered into thoughts of what his life might be like if he had just gone to Pasadena Junior College, gotten married, and sold insurance or something, like so many of his high school classmates. Sometimes he spoke of "not really relating to Yale and the Ivy League syndrome." Part of the dark, conflicted side.

Paul Hoffman did not really take to Brad, although he spent quite a bit of time hanging around with us, bringing his "monarchist friends" around for port and cigars. Hoffman was to say later, not kindly, that "Brad Bishop did not fit in at Yale. He was from a different background. Manner not Yale. Funny hairstyle." All of which was very snobbish and narrow of Hoffman, who might just as well have been unconsciously describing himself. But, most alarmingly, he went on to say that "Bishop had been in an anarchistic clique at Yale." What nonsense! Where did Hoffman make that up? Had I formed "an anarchistic clique?" Certainly not! And Brad and I never discussed anarchy, or even any sentiments that might have been construed disloyal to either the United States government or the society that we were a part of. Except for some of that "existentialist despair." Which was abstract, mostly.

Brad and I often played squash in one of the two under-used courts in the basement of Calhoun College. Brad had not been a squash player but he quickly picked up the game and some of its intricacy. I also was not a squash player. Each of us had played tennis, and while that is quite different from squash, at least one has a notion of how to hold a racket and hit a ball. Our games were all the same. We would start out evenly matched, and then Brad would inch ahead and win the match by a point or two. I strove mightily to defeat him, but never could. Noticing my frustration, one day Brad said to me, "You have to face it, man—I am just better than you." Meaning at squash—but perhaps in general. Who knows? There was a sort of arrogance that lurked beneath Brad's easy-going surface, along with doubt and darkness. I sometimes detected these conflicting qualities, and one time declared him to be "a curious mixture of good guy and poet." The poet part being darkness and doubt, of course.

One time I took Brad along on one of my weekend visits to Cambridge, Massachusetts, where I was in the habit of visiting the attractive daughter of a Harvard professor. On this particular weekend there was a lot of gaiety and socializing, and Brad was very comfortable with everything, He charmed my friend and her girlfriends with his sort of laid back semi-macho folksiness. I could suddenly see that he was quite the ladies man—since Yale was so monastic there was little socializing with the opposite sex. All in all, it was a very pleasant weekend. We both agreed that Cambridge was a far more worldly environment than New Haven, but the many distractions probably would have done us in. But, I was interested to see that "happy-go-lucky," social side of Brad.

As graduation approached Brad discussed with me his dilemma about marrying Annette. Whenever he asked for my opinion, which not often, I simply told him that it was a matter only he could decide. He seemed very ambivalent about it. Brad did not have a clear view of his future. He said that he might join the army, to see what was going on "in the real world." I don't think that Brad had much of a feel for Yale and his time there. Once he said, "I've been here for four years, and now it's time to get the hell out." I think that he thought of Yale as just a place and stage in his life. He said that his parents were coming to the graduation ceremonies. Annette would be coming also, and I would have the opportunity to meet her.

When graduation finally did arrive, I barely did more than say hello to Brad's parents. And my introduction to Annette was very brief indeed. I was surprised that I did not find her to be what I thought a Southern California high school cheer-leader would be. Of course, I had stereotypes, but they were based on the real thing from my experience. I found Annette to be something on the plain side. But nice.

It seemed to me odd when I heard that later that summer Brad had indeed married Annette in South Pasadena—and joined the army the very next day! And I found it odder still when I was informed by Dr. Avis (as Lionel Alves had come to be called) from the army's Language Institute in Monterey, California, that Brad Bishop was also there, seemingly with a very elite group of guys and studying Serbo-Croatian. Who had heard of that? Well, obviously people in Yugoslavia had. But who else? Why would the army be teaching recruits like Brad something like that? In retrospect I think the army had some special role in mind for Brad Bishop. Something to do with Yugoslavia. Thinking on it, Brad had a distinctive look that could very well have been Serbian. That look those people have.

After Yale I did not keep in touch with Brad. So it came as a surprise when he wrote to me care of my father's place in Malibu in the fall of 1964, asking if I was going to be in southern California at Thanksgiving. And, if so, might we possibly get together? As we have seen in the previous chapter, we did. As for Serbo-Croatian, well something seemed to be developing along that line also...

III.

THE STORY OF MARIA BEGOVIC

I am here going to engage in a digression from the mainstream of the Bishop story. The reader may find this digression not pertinent, as it has to do with Yugoslavia, with Croatia to be exact. The reader will remember that I was told by a Yale classmate who had served in Europe with U.S. Army Intelligence, and who had known Bishop there, that "Bishop was running a guy in Yugoslavia." So, this slight digression may have some pertinence, as will hopefully be demonstrated later on.

In the mid-1980s when I was the first Director of the Sonoma County Museum in Santa Rosa, California, we had amongst our large and important group of volunteers one Maria Begovic. She was a rather nondescript woman of perhaps seventy years of age, with a European accent, and a rather retiring manner. I took her to be a widow, as were so many of our female volunteers. I only knew her to smile and nod at, as I did with all the volunteers, important as they were to the functioning of the museum.

At some point the Sonoma County Museum arranged for its volunteers a trip to the DeYoung Museum in San Francisco for a luncheon and a tour of a special exhibit. It was suggested by our Board of Directors that I accompany this group to the DeYoung. As a "show of solidarity," so to speak. I had a reputation for being somewhat aloof and formal. This experience, it was thought, would "humanize" me. Well, maybe…

Boarding the bus in Santa Rosa I found a vacant seat. It was next to Maria Begovic. As we rolled south through Marin County she and I chatted pleasantly about inconsequential matters. The museum, her volunteer work, Santa Rosa, how long had she been there? She had a good idiomatic command of the English language, even if her accent was a bit pronounced. I wondered what European country she might be from. I guessed a Slavic one, because of the "ic" ending of her name.

It was not until just before crossing the Golden Gate Bridge that I asked her flat out, "What country are you originally from, Maria?" She looked at me for a minute, then said quickly, "I am from Yugoslavia— from Croatia, actually. We had to escape from there after World War Two. Three days over the mountains to Austria. In the snow. Sometimes barefoot. It was awful. But we had to get away from the Communists." She fell silent, looking out the bus window. I said, "Communists? Serbs?" She turned back and said sharply, "Yes, Serbs. Serbs— All gypsies! Communists!" "Of course," I mumbled. Then she went on, "Croatia is not gypsies. European country. Like Austria. Roman Catholic, not Slav. But what you care, you probably never heard of Croatia." I smiled and said, "I Solisti di Zagreb." She smiled. "World famous." I added, "And then there is Zvonomir the First, last King of Croatia, who ruled from 1075 to 1089—discounting of course that pretender to the throne, Petrus." Now Maria really looked at me wide-eyed. "How you know that? Zvonomir very great man. Considered father of Croatia. How you know about him?"

I laughed and told Maria that at Yale University one of my good friends was a student of Eastern European and Balkan History. And that one night when a group of us were out drinking someone had asked, "Who we gonna dedicate this round to?" And my friend said, out of the blue, "We drink to Zvonomir the First, last King of Croatia, who ruled from 1075 to 1089—discounting that pretender to the throne, Petrus…" Everybody thought it was a splendid toast, and all glasses were raised. I told Maria it was nothing more than an idle toast to a medieval king. She seemed appeased, somewhat. But still looking at me rather curiously.

Then I said something that in retrospect I probably should not have mentioned. I said to Maria, "Of course, in more modern times there is Ante Pavelic." She really looked at me wide-eyed. "How you know about him?" she almost shouted. Rather agitated. "Just from reading history," I said. She snorted and spat out, "Ante Pavelic—a most misunderstood man…" There was a long silence. Finally, as we were nearing the DeYoung Museum, I commented, "Yes, yes. Most misunderstood. Just a Croatian patriot, trying to help his people." "Yes, yes, yes…"Maria agreed quickly, looking at me as if to detect any note of irony in either my voice or manner. I hoped there was none, but I knew that Ante Pavelic was not a simple patriot, but the "Poglavnic of Croatia"—Hitler's hand-picked thug and a very nasty piece of work. Much misunderstood indeed…

Maria hurried off the bus and did not sit anywhere near me during the luncheon. She seemed to avoid me while we toured the exhibit. And likewise on the return trip. She sat at the front of the bus, well away from me. I planned, when we reached Santa Rosa, to seek her out and tell her how much I had enjoyed her company, etc. But not to be. I barely caught sight of her scurrying away. Did the fact that I knew a few things about Croatia upset her? If so, why? She had been away from that country, from the gypsies, for forty years. Let go! But, as we have come to know, Balkan memories are long…

I did not give Maria Begovic any more thought. Just another neurotic volunteer. I had already met a few of those. I wished that our volunteers were younger and more vivacious. But that was not the way it was.

About three days after the bus excursion my secretary asked if I would see volunteer Maria Begovic. What now? I wondered. Maria entered my office and I gestured for her to be seated across from my desk (which was large and imposing). She seemed very nervous and ill at ease. I asked her what was on her mind, and she burst out with a string of declarations that were hard to understand. I told her to calm down and tell me very slowly what was bothering her.

"Oh, Mr. Lummis, I have barely slept in three nights. I have been so upset, so worried. I am thinking, Mr. Lummis, how does he know these things about my country, about Croatia? I am thinking, Mr. Lummis must be CIA!" I was simply astounded, and told Maria so. I told her that I was just a simple museum director who had a friend in college who had told him a few things about Croatia and that is all. Simply preposterous to think I was CIA! How could she possibly be thinking that? Maria kept shaking her head, and blowing her nose with a Kleenex. I got her calmed down by repeating over and over again how absurd it was to think that Museum Director Lummis might be CIA! I think some of that did sink in, because she left my office somewhat calmer and apologizing for "thinking such things."

This time I did some thinking about what might be bothering Maria Begovic, refugee from Croatia, believer that Ante Pavelic was/is only "a much misunderstood man." There was something dark hidden there, some dark Croatian nationalism. Nazism even. She had been involved in something, been a part of something, had done something, somewhere along the line that caused this paranoia about CIA. Perhaps even something ongoing, current.

But, not my problem. I had a museum to run…

Later, however, when I came to know something about Croatia, Ante Pavelic, the Ustache, Croatian nationalism—and Brad Bishop—I would reflect on Maria Begovic and her paranoia. There was something there. Something that reached out and stretched over the years. Balkan memories are long…

I related the tale of Maria Begovic to Dr. Avis, who was living at that time in San Francisco and working part time for Jim Ferrigan's "International Flag Store." He was interested in the story, and mentioned that Croatians in the Bay Area from time to time came into the store to order flags. Their requests were usually for the current Croatian national flag, but the Doctor said that occasionally there were somewhat unusual requests, usually for flags shown in old photographs: monarchy, nobility, nationalist groups, etc. Sometimes these flags were a bit sinister, with less than wholesome connotations, occasionally having to do with the Nazi period, the Ustache. The Doctor knew this both as a historian of Eastern Europe and a vexillologist (flag expert.) The store was always glad to have these flags made, no questions asked.

Occasionally the Doctor attempted some relevant conversation with the Croatians, perhaps something about their flag. He said that they always shut up right away. They were very paranoid and always paid in cash. He suspected strongly that the names they supplied for their flag orders were fake. He also had the feeling that there were Croatian right-wing nationalist (Nazi?) organizations in the Bay Area, and elsewhere in the country.

He said that Maria Begovic's paranoia was quite understandable...

IV.

THE DETECTIVE CALLS

In the winter of 1997-98 I was on a visit in Pennsylvania. One evening Paul Hoffman called from his isolated converted school house in western Chester County. He said, "There is going to be a TV show on Brad Bishop later this week, Thursday night. Come on out for our annual winter tour of the Amish country, then we can come back and watch this show. It's *America's Most Wanted*, or something." I had seen a couple of the so-called Bishop shows on Meredith's machine, but evidently Hoffman had not. He seemed excited.

So, on the appointed day I drove out to Hoffman's place. Our tour of the Amish country included one of the huge buffets of Pennsylvania Dutch offerings that are found in Lancaster County. The experience always leaves me somewhat uneasy, both physically and psychologically. So it was a relief to get back to Hoffman's place, an old school house at the end of a two mile dirt road, that his parents had many years before converted into a summer retreat. Hoffman constructed a fire and we settled into big leather chairs to talk about the Bishop case and await the program. As mentioned, I had seen a couple of these programs, which followed basically the same format: a recapitulation of the crime, some

background on Bishop, and then commentary by
law enforcement types. Ending with emphasis on
anywhere in the world, etc. Not terribly edifying.

The program that Hoffman and I watched that evening was not
substantially much different, except that it did present some fairly
interesting "home movies" or videos of the Bishop family. I thought
Annette seemed much more attractive than I remembered. There were
shots of the crime scene. One that interested me showed the bathroom
door that had been kicked in at the bottom. It appeared to be a flimsy,
hollow core door. Something about that struck me as incongruous.
More on that later. Hoffman was all wound up after the program. With
all sorts of theories, none of which made much sense. He said that he
was going to contact the TV network to request a copy of the tape, so
he could watch it over and over again, studying it. I thought that would
be a waste of time, but I knew that Hoffman had much time to waste.
So I agreed that he should contact the network and see if he could get
a copy of the program tape. Essentially, the crux of the matter was that
Bishop was long gone. Where he might be, nobody had the slightest
clue. Nothing to add to that.

Before I left that night to drive back to St David's I told Hoffman
a story that I found interesting. It was something that Dr. Avis (the
former Lionel Alves, Yale 1959 and a good friend) had told me. It seems
that a year or so before the good Doctor had been traveling in Mexico.
One day when he was visiting Veracruz he had some reason to visit the
United States consulate to get answers to some minor questions. While
in the reception area of the consulate office he noticed, on a bulletin
board, a rather prominently displayed "wanted poster" for William
Bradford Bishop, Jr., in Spanish. When he asked the secretary about
it, she replied animatedly, "Oh, señor, he is a very bad man. He has
killed more people in your country..." Just as she was saying that, the
consul came out of his office and quickly corrected her, saying that
she had it wrong, that Bishop had not killed any more people, at least

.ot to anyone's knowledge. In the consul's office, before getting to his own questions, the Doctor asked about the Spanish language wanted poster. Did the authorities think Bishop might be in Mexico or South America? "I don't really know." said the consul, "The State Department routinely sends wanted posters like that to consulates. Just in case, you know…" There seemed to be nothing more to be learned about the matter, so the Doctor turned to his own questions. Later, when he told me this story, we agreed that there was probably nothing to it. Just that a lot fugitives headed to South America, particularly Brazil where there was no extradition treaty, or maybe Paraguay where a lot of ex-Nazis seemed to be "hiding" rather openly. No reason to think that Bishop might not be among them. (The fugitives, that is, not the Nazis—but perhaps among them as well…) I seemed to remember that among his language skills Spanish was listed.

Hoffman did not seem very interested in any of this stuff about Veracruz. He was still too pumped up about the TV program. It seemed that he was hardly listening when I told him about the Doctor's story.

Not long after the Doctor told me about his experience in Veracruz, I had an odd dream. In it I could see Bishop very clearly, working at a ski resort somewhere, with lots of snow around. He was assisting people on and off a chair lift, smiling, and being extremely helpful and affable. That was all. There were ski resorts in Chile, were there not? But somehow I thought the locale to be in a northern clime. Switzerland, perhaps. Well, just a dream. But how had hot and steamy Veracruz prompted some notion of Bishop working in a ski resort? I guessed that there was no connection. Dreams happen…

A few days after I returned to Santa Fe, one evening the telephone rang. When I answered a gruff voice asked, "Is this Dayton Lummis?" I said that it was, and inquired as to who was calling and why. I heard, "This is Detective Cady of the Montgomery County, Maryland, Sheriff's Department. What's this bullshit about Brad Bishop killing more people?" I asked where he had heard that. He told me, "I just talked to your buddy Hoffman. He had contacted the TV network to ask for a copy of that recent Bishop program, and they pass on such information to us—just in case there might be something. Anyway, he said that you told him that some pal of yours heard in Mexico that Bishop has killed more people. What's that about?" I told the detective that Hoffman had not got things quite right, that he had not been paying attention. Then, I proceeded to tell the detective the story just as Dr. Avis had told it to me. The detective seemed satisfied. I asked him about that wanted poster in the consulate in Spanish. He hesitated, then said, "Well, we think he might be in South America." Why South America? I asked. Sightings? Other information? The detective was vague, saying only that a lot of perps head for South America. He would not get more specific than that. So I began to ask some questions about the case. He was quite talkative. When I asked if there was any doubt as to Bishop's guilt (Why had I begun wondering about that?), he answered with great finality, "Absolutely NOT!" When could Bishop last be proven in a court of law to be alive? When he signed the credit card slip in the sporting goods store in North Carolina. Had the Feds been cooperative in the case? This was met with what I call a great snort of derision, "HAH!" I wondered about that. There was some more superficial discussion, wherein I learned nothing more than what had been in the newspapers or on the TV shows. I finally got around to the matter of Bishop's vehicle being found in a parking lot on the western side of Great Smoky Mountains National Park. Did the detective have any theory or explanation for that? He did, and went on to tell me some things about that matter. That the authorities had ruled out Bishop going deep into the forest and committing suicide. Bloodhounds had been brought in. The dogs followed Bishop's trail about a mile into the forest, where it stopped. It did not branch off into the woods. Just stopped. The theory was that Bishop had walked that far, then turned around and gone back to the parking lot. Where the dogs followed his trail to a sort of bulletin board on which were posted maps of the park, trails, features, rules and regulations, things like that. Then the trail went out into the middle of the parking lot, which was empty at that time of year, and stopped. Stopped? Yes, stopped, the detective told me. Indicating that at that spot Bishop had gotten into a vehicle. "Somebody picked the-son-of-a-bitch up, helped him get away!" Who? I asked. How could that happen? The detective said that the authorities had no idea, no leads, nothing. Just that somebody helped him to get away. Or, I thought, perhaps something else, something that the authorities did not care to speculate on. To them the case was cut and dried. Bishop killed five family members and was a fugitive. He would be apprehended. The detective indicated that a likely path of flight would have been south to the Mexican border, where one could at that time cross into that country virtually unchecked—that was 1976. Which probably led to the South America theory. But—so many years later?

We talked a bit more about the case, the likelihood of Bishop being captured. More than twenty years had passed since the crimes. No more recent sightings. Bishop could be anywhere, said the detective. Dead, even. That's a possibility.

A few days later Hoffman called me to ask if I had heard from the detective. When I told him that I had, he seemed pleased. Like he had taken an important role in the investigation. When I told him that the information that he had given the detective was all botched up he seemed deflated.

In the meantime, I read an interesting novel based on the Bishop case, *The Darkroom*, by Carolyn Banks. Not a first rate piece of work, but one with an intriguing theory about the murders and how (Bishop) could have lived with himself in the aftermath, constructing a new life and so forth. Worth reading, if one is interested in this case.

V.

RECONSTRUCTION

In this chapter I am going to present all aspects of the Bishop case as they appeared in the print media. Collected from what I have been able to have access to, mostly from the Internet, the archives of *The Washington Post* and *The New York Times*, and various and assorted other published sources. I will deal with the stories exactly as they appeared. If there are conflicting details, these will be so noted. But, I will ask no questions, make no judgments, offer no theories. All that will come later.

I will deal with five separate aspects of the crime: the grave discovery site; the murder scene; the murders themselves; flight; and aftermath, including comments, questions, notions as reported in the press.

Tyrrell County, North Carolina, lies in the northeastern part of the state, sandy and swampy, heavily forested with pine and oak, somewhat inland from the Outer Banks. It is the state's least populated county, with just about four thousand citizens. The industries, if they can be so called, are logging and fishing. A CIA "training facility" is rumored to be hidden away somewhere in the thick forests, but there is no absolute verification of that. There is some sort of "facility" on the north side of Albemarle Sound, at Point David in another county. No major highways enter the county, and by any stretch of the imagination Tyrrell County can be considered a very out-of-the-way place.

At about ten in the morning of 2 March 1976 a spotter in the Scotia Fire Tower about five miles south of Columbia, the 900 resident county seat of Tyrrell County, spotted wisps of smoke rising from the pine forest just off State Highway 94, about one mile southeast of the tower. The spotter contacted state forest ranger Ronald Brickhouse and instructed him to investigate. Driving slowly off the state highway on a narrow and sandy logging road the ranger came to a small fire, about three acres, burning slowly, or smoldering because of dampness from a night of heavy fog. The burn was about one half mile from the nearest residence. The ranger got his tools from his truck and began working to put out the perimeters of the fire. At some point he decided to investigate what he took to be a shallow depression at the center of the burned area. He saw what he took to be the bodies of some discarded hogs, but when he drew closer he was shocked to find human bodies in a shallow trench roughly six feet by four feet. The bodies had been lightly singed and very slightly covered with dirt. Ranger Brickhouse later told reporters, "When you walk up expecting to see hogs and find people, your belly really goes..." Near to the gravesite was a slightly burned two and one-half gallon gas can (other reports mentioned a five-gallon can), a shovel and an old pitchfork. The very upset ranger ran to his truck and contacted by radio the two-man sheriff's department (sheriff and one deputy) in nearby Columbia and reported the gruesome find.

The two Tyrrell County lawmen arrived quickly, secured the scene and removed the bodies from the depression. Determining that a brutal homicide had taken place they covered the bodies with a tarp and contacted the North Carolina State Police, realizing that they were not equal to dealing with a crime of such enormity. While waiting for the State Police the two lawmen examined the area for possible evidence, careful to not disturb anything, especially the gas can and the two tools. Ranger Brickhouse was released from the scene as soon as the small fire was out. "I was scared," the ranger said, thinking that perhaps the murderer might still be in the area.

North Carolina State Police arrived and took charge, followed by fifteen agents from the State Bureau of Criminal Investigation. They examined the bodies—a middle-aged woman, an older woman, and three young males. The three males had towels wrapped around bloody heads. There was no identification on the bodies. The Tyrrell County sheriff, Royce Rhodes, stated that the deceased were not local people because he knew every resident of Tyrrell County. Dr. Page Hudson, the state medical examiner, determined that all five had suffered mortal extreme blunt force to the head. Impressions were taken of tire tracks in the damp soft earth near the gravesite. The gas can and tools were taken as evidence. There was nothing else. The bodies were removed to a lab in Chapel Hill for further examination and attempts at identification. The only clue was that some of the woman's clothing bore labels from high-end shops in the Washington D.C. area.

Sometime during the day of the discovery, a nearby resident came forth to state that early that morning he had come upon a maroon Chevy station wagon exiting from that forest area at what he took to be an unusually rapid rate of speed. Indeed, the bodies seemed hastily and carelessly buried, and the attempt to burn them quite inefficient. All indicating perhaps extreme haste. As if in fear of being discovered. The singed gas can indicated to investigators the possibility of it having ignited, perhaps burning the perpetrator.

For six days the bodies remained unidentified, and there was no movement in the case. Then...

The shovel found at the gravesite had on it's handle a manufacturer's label. Through that, investigators were able to trace the shovel to a suburban Maryland hardware store where the item had been sold sometime a year or two earlier. Acting on a hunch the authorities assembled a poster of the victims as tastefully as possible, with the hope that by posting it in the hardware store someone might recognize the individuals. And indeed, someone did. A young girl who had babysat for the Bishop family gasped when looking at the poster and exclaimed, "My God—those are the Bishops!"

The fact that there had been no one noticed in or around the Bishop family house for a week or more had not struck any of the neighbors as odd. There had been talk in school by the boys of a skiing trip. But after almost a week, one of the boys' teachers attempted to contact the mother. Several phone calls went unanswered without arousing any suspicions. Finally a neighbor began to wonder if perhaps something might be wrong. She found the house locked and seemingly deserted, but detected what she thought might be blood stains on the front steps leading to the entry door. She contacted police, who gained entry to the house and immediately became aware of a potential crime scene. The Bishop family was evidently missing.

Aware of the information on five bodies found in a shallow grave in North Carolina, Montgomery County Sheriff's Department contacted the authorities in that state. It quickly became apparent that the victims in the shallow grave were the five members of the Bishop family. And William Bradford Bishop, Jr., was missing.

Having identified the five bodies in the shallow grave in North Carolina as members of the Bishop family, and having entered the Bishop home (a four-bedroom, split-level $100,000 house in the middle-class Carderock Springs section of Bethesda, Maryland, a suburb of Washington, D.C.) and identifying it as an evident crime scene, and with William Bradford Bishop, Jr., missing, on March 8 the authorities quite understandably named Bishop "a person of interest." Of very great interest one might say.

The crime scene at the Bishop house was described in somewhat differing terms:

1. A detective entered the house and found blood splattered on the floor. Going up the stairs to the second level he found more blood splatterings on the walls and floor. "And then, as if it could not get any

worse, as the detective entered what were believed to be the rooms of the three young boys, he found that the entire rooms were covered with blood, ceiling to floor, wall to wall. The detective stated that in twelve years as an officer it was the worst scene he had ever seen."

2. In four bedrooms of the Bishop home, and on the stairs and landing by the front door, police discovered blotchy splatters of blood. Otherwise, they said, there were no signs of forced entry or physical violence. Corporal Philip Caswell stated, "There was no struggle in the home, as far as we can tell…"

With what information the police had so far, they set to work to attempt to recreate the crime as it unfolded on March 1.

On that date William Bradford Bishop, Jr. was a ten year employee of the United States Department of State, with the rather cumbersome title of "Assistant Chief of Special Trade Activities and Commercial Treaties Division" in the Office of International Trade in the State Department's Bureau of Economics and Business Affairs. He had been appointed to that position, Grade 4, with an annual salary of $25,962, in 1971. He had been in the position somewhat longer than was normal but "not unusual." By the first of March 1976 he was being considered for a promotion.

Evidently, that morning Bishop learned that he had been passed over for the hoped-for promotion. By late afternoon he told his secretary that he was feeling "unwell, perhaps coming down with the flu," and left at 5:30 p.m., considered "early" for him. It can be proven that he drove from the State Department offices at "Foggy Bottom" to the Montgomery Mall, a commercial center in suburban Maryland not far from his house. At a Sears, Roebuck store there he purchased, with his Bank of America credit card—the only one he possessed—a two and one half gallon metal gasoline can (sometimes described erroneously as a five-gallon can) and a four pound, short handled "sledgehammer" (sometimes described as "a heavy ball peen hammer.") Following these purchases he went to a Texaco station in the vicinity and bought fifteen gallons of gasoline, including at least two gallons poured into the metal can, "the FBI reported." Four Texaco stations in the vicinity were questioned, but no attendants could remember anything about any such purchase or individual. (This information comes from a Texaco credit purchase receipt that was discovered somewhat later.) Then, at a nearby branch of Bank of America he withdrew $400 "from a savings account."

Bishop evidently arrived home at or about 6:30 p.m., as at that time "a neighbor caught a glimpse of him outside his house." The Bishops had lived in the neighborhood for about three years, but were not close with their neighbors. Investigators initially believed that the murders were initiated shortly after that time, but soon changed the time to approximately 11 p.m. based on evidence that will be discussed a bit farther along.

Investigators theorized that Annette Bishop was attacked and killed first, as she sat reading in the den on the first or ground floor level, where a book was found lying on the floor. They surmise that the killer was surprised by the return of Lobelia Bishop, who had been out walking the family dog Leo, a Golden Retriever, a ritual that, according to neighbors, took place each night at approximately 11 p.m. The killer evidently quickly attempted to conceal the body of his victim by covering it with one or two coats. But, think the investigators, Lobelia Bishop somehow immediately realized that something was most terribly wrong, dropped the dog's leash and ran upstairs where she locked herself in a bathroom. The killer evidently pursued her, kicked open the door to the bathroom and beat her to death in that space. (A television special on the Bishop case showed a hollow core door kicked in at the bottom,) Then the killer proceeded to kill the three sleeping boys, delivering one or more powerful blows to their heads as they lay in their beds. The coroner indicated that the murder instrument was a blunt object, believed to be the short handled hammer that Bishop had purchased earlier that day. This object was never found. There was a poker missing from the fireplace, and that, too, was never found. *The Washington Post* published a crude diagram of the three levels of the house, indicating where each body had been found, the wife in the den, the mother in the bathroom, one boy alone in one upstairs bedroom, and the two others in another upstairs bedroom.

After the murders the killer evidently wrapped each body in a blanket or rug and half carried and half dragged them down stairs to the front door. (Bloody drag marks were found.) Then, in a similar manner the bodies were transported down thirteen cement slabs to the driveway and the waiting Chevy station wagon. Evidence of blood was found on those slabs, which were removed as evidence. Inside the house the investigators did find some faint bloody finger and hand prints on walls which were subjected to examination for possible identification.

With the bodies in the car, the killer evidently retrieved the dog Leo and placed him in the car. No dog was reported running loose in the neighborhood. He then began the long drive of 300 miles to the spot in North Carolina which was evidently his immediate destination. The trip would have taken six plus hours and would have taken the vehicle through several toll booths. That time line fits the sighting of a vehicle matching Bishop's that was seen in the vicinity of the graves early in the morning of March 2.

North Carolina authorities revealed that they had been able to recover one good fingerprint from the gasoline can found at the gravesite. This was revealed to be Bishop's. At first police stated that they did not have sufficient evidence to issue a warrant for Bishop's arrest. Then, the bloody prints at the house were identified as belonging to Bishop. This evidence, plus the fact that Bishop had withdrawn $400 from his savings account and was missing and believed to be a fugitive, convinced the authorities to issue a warrant for his arrest on March 12. The FBI swiftly followed with a warrant for apprehension on a charge of interstate flight to avoid prosecution, etc. Bishop was officially a fugitive and a suspect in the murders of his family.

Extensive search, land and air, of the gravesite region revealed nothing. Then, tracking Bishop's possible credit card use, a report came in that Bishop's Bank of America credit card had been used late in the day on March 2, the day the bodies were discovered, to make a purchase of $15.60 at a sporting goods store in Jacksonville, North Carolina, a medium sized coastal town about one hundred miles south of the gravesite by circuitous routes. Handwriting analysis proved Bishop had signed the form, and that he had definitely been in the store making a purchase the day the bodies were found, between 5 and 7 p.m.

At first employees of the store—described both as "Outside Sports Store" and "Bobby Simpson's Sporting Goods"—could not remember the sale or anyone making a purchase for that amount during those hours. After further examination of the transaction slip it was thought that the purchase was for "tennis shoes."

The store owner, John Wheatly, was summoned to the premises. His analysis was that the purchase was for "sporting goods," more than one item, perhaps a sweat shirt and athletic socks. Another report was that the item purchased was "a dog leash." In another the store owner remembered the transaction because the customer "was wearing a suit, a thing very damned few of my customers would wear." When shown pictures of Bishop, Wheatly said that the individual "seemed awfully familiar," that it was the customer he remembered. Who, he said had been polite and well-spoken. He remembered that the man "had been with a dark skinned woman." (In the South "dark skinned" does not mean "black" or "Negro," but just what it says. Like Mexican or Central American.) In this case Wheatly went on to clarify the woman as "Caribbean looking," and was either inside the store holding the dog on a leash while Bishop paid, or waiting outside holding the dog on a leash. He said that they definitely "seemed like a couple, they were definitely together. I don't know why the police didn't focus on that woman earlier…"

A second report came in a few days later from Wilmington, North Carolina, about fifty miles on down the coast from Jacksonville. A waitress, Barbara James, at the Kettle Pancake house reported that a man came in about midnight on Wednesday March 2 who had evidently been drinking. She said, "You are trained to get a real good look at potential trouble makers." She described the man as about 40, medium height with brown hair. He grabbed her arm and offered $2 for her to seat him right away. He was abusive to some black men seated in a nearby booth, calling them "niggers" and other abusive terms. (That would have been out of character for Bishop, it was reported, who had worked all over Africa and got along well with blacks.) The black men got up, telling the man to "shut his mouth." Barbara James told the cooks that there might be a fight, but the black men walked out angrily. The man sat down, ordered sausage and eggs, and continued to be obnoxious, grabbing the waitress's arm. Finally he finished, paid $1.80, left a $1 tip, said he had to get back on the road and headed to the men's room. Barbara James reported the man's behavior to two plain clothes Sheriff's detectives who had come into the restaurant, and one of them, Wiggins, went to the men's room to check on the man, but found that he had left by the back door. The next day Wiggins came back to the restaurant with some photographs of Bishop which he showed to Barbara James. She said, "That was him all right." When told that he was wanted for the murder of his family, she exclaimed, "I could have fallen through the floor!" The two detectives also were sure that the man in the restaurant had been Bishop. Several other people around Wilmington reported seeing a man resembling the photographs of Bishop that had been in the local paper. The manager of a local Citgo gas station said on Thursday a "reddish Chevy station with Maryland plates" had been the station. Intensive surveillance around the Wilmington area turned up no sight or any other reports of anyone resembling Bishop, or any sightings of a reddish station wagon with Maryland plates.

The individual who created the scene in the Wilmington restaurant was indeed a man who very much resembled Bishop, but who was in reality a crewman who had been on shore leave from a tanker docked at Atlantic Beach that had been transporting fertilizer. Other sightings in the region proved to be either erroneous or mistaken.

Bishop's diplomatic passport was missing from both his office and his house, indicating that he might use it to travel anywhere in the world. But, the owner's registration for the Chevy station was found at the house. One detective observed that without that he could not legally sell the vehicle. But he could "run it into a river or swamp. Or just abandon it somewhere."

Which is just what happened.

Elkmont Campground was a private facility on the west side of Great Smoky Mountains National Park, not far from Gatlinburg, Tennessee. The location was some four hundred miles west of the location in eastern North Carolina where the Bishop family bodies had been found. There were some cabins owned by wealthy persons from Knoxville, and a few cabins lived in year round by persons who maintained the other cabins and the facility, and did various odd jobs. Generally during the winter months it is a damp, cold and rather lonely spot. On the 18th of March few of these people began to get suspicious of a reddish Chevy station wagon that had been parked in a lot next to a stream "for at least two weeks." Rather too long for recreationalists at that time of year. They notified Park personnel who towed the vehicle to a Park maintenance lot. There it was determined that the station wagon belonged to William Bradford Bishop, Jr., who was wanted in the State of Maryland on five charges of capital murder.

Almost immediately a team of thirty FBI agents and state and local law enforcement officials swept down on the scene. A massive air and land search was initiated, with agents and bloodhounds searching every mountain trail and back road for miles around. A search of the vehicle revealed the following: a spare tire well with evidence of a substantial amount of blood having been present; several blood-stained blankets; an ax with a long handle (determined to have not been the murder weapon); dog biscuits; a twelve gauge Mossberg bolt action shotgun in a case and a box of ammunition; a man's sport coat and a man's overcoat; a suitcase with man's clothing and toilet articles; two canvas tarps. The vehicle had 17,711 miles on the odometer, and the tank was three quarters full. (Gas purchase(s) must have been with cash.)

In the glove box agents found a Texaco receipt for fifteen gallons of gas (believed to have been purchased the afternoon before the killings); Maps of North Carolina and Tennessee; city maps of Atlanta and Miami; and two empty vials labeled Serax, a drug similar to Valium that the FBI learned had been prescribed for Bishop by a psychiatrist. At first the FBI thought "For depression and possible suicidal tendencies." This was challenged by several psychiatrists who indicated that it was a low level drug with no significant withdrawal symptoms. And that without it a person could function moderately well, but would do better with it and could not refill the prescription without a doctor's official form.

Based on the initial analysis agents theorized that Bishop might have gone deep into the mountains and committed suicide, his body being eaten by bears and coyotes and the bones scattered about. But, this theory did not stand up, for a number of reasons. It was felt that having gone through with the murders, the transporting and attempted burning of the bodies, the subject would be "too desensitized" to feel sufficient remorse to take his life. Further, no evidence could be found of Bishop entering into the mountain forests, though it was certainly possible. (Oddly, there was no mention of Detective Cady's explanation of the dogs following a scent one mile up a trail and back again, then circling in the parking lot where it stopped—the implication being that Bishop had entered a car at that point.)

The only information about the vehicle and its possible occupant came from two men who were year round residents of the campground. T. Higden was a caretaker of the cabins and a watchman. He said that the vehicle had arrived about ten days to two weeks prior to March 18, probably the 5th or 6th of March, he thought, between 12 noon and 3:30 p.m., the times when he habitually made his rounds. Steve Ownby was working with his father on a cabin they were building two days after he had first noticed the station wagon (March 5th or 6th), thinking it belonged to campers or fishermen. He noticed that "a sandy haired man wearing a blue parka and jeans stumbled by" the site where he was working. He said the man "looked tired, and was real, real dirty, with a week's growth of beard." He dismissed him as a drifter, of the type that occasionally passed through the area, usually on foot.

The FBI had not given up on the idea that Bishop had taken to the mountains, to hide and eventually escape. Agent Harold Swanson said, "If he knew the area real well, from previous camping expeditions, had the proper equipment, depending on his mental state, he could stay hidden in those mountains for quite some time." Soon thinking came around to the notion that he had left the park just after the car had been abandoned, around the 5th or 6th of March. It was thought that hitching a ride out of the park to some city would not be difficult. That would give Bishop a two-week head start. On the 29th of March back in Maryland a Grand Jury indicted William Bradford Bishop, Jr. on five counts of capital murder.

One more tidbit was of interest to the agents. A group of boy scouts said that they had met up with a couple from Cleveland who were on their way hitch-hiking to Florida. This couple told the scouts that the night before, March 6th, they had camped with a man in street clothes who was carrying a duffle bag. The man seemed to know the country and said he was on his way to Newfound Gap. Agents were unable to locate the hitchhiking couple, nor at Newfound Gap were they able to immediately locate any mountain hiker in street clothes. After a bit they were able to interview a somewhat eccentric North Carolina man who was known to wander in the mountains. It was determined that this was the man in street clothes and with a duffle bag that the couple had seen.

The hunt for the fugitive was called off. Special Agent Swanson conceded that "it seems that the trail ended when he stepped out of that vehicle." There was no trace, either, of the dog.

There was one further report that brought a flurry of interest. The owner of a gun shop in Rutherford, North Carolina, about 60 miles to the east of the Great Smoky search region, on March 20 told a *Washington Post* reporter that a week earlier, on March 12 a man fitting Bishop's description had flashed a State Department identification card in his store in an attempt to trade a loaded .38 caliber pistol for a more powerful magnum handgun. The store owner, who asked not to be identified, said that he refused to swap weapons, or to sell another gun because "the guy was waving a loaded gun around in my store!" He described the man as middle aged, about six feet tall with sandy hair. The man said, "He was wearing a rumpled suit and looked very tired." When he saw Bishop's picture in the paper a few days later he passed his information to his local police department, who notified the North Carolina State Bureau of Investigation and the FBI. These agencies sent men to Rutherford, with bloodhounds, but neither their investigation nor the dogs turned up any indication that Bishop had been in the store or the immediate area. A FBI spokesman said, "We have no reason to doubt the store owner who reported the incident. He told us what he saw. But the dogs we took there (for scent tracing) showed no reaction. We have nothing about Bishop since we found his car."

At first investigators could find absolutely no motive or reason for the brutal murders that Bishop allegedly committed. Then, a few items began to surface, nothing major, but indicators nonetheless. There were mentions of some mild financial problems, some very low level marital distress—Annette objected to travel and moving to strange places while Bishop thrived on that—and tension caused by the overbearing mother-in-law. And of course, the missed promotion. Small things, doubtless, and not generally the sorts of things that would drive a man to brutally murder his entire family.

And, it was learned from the vials of Serax found in the abandoned car, that Bishop had been seeing a psychiatrist for depression and possible alcoholism. The FBI thought that without the drug Bishop might have severe withdrawal problems (That opinion was later downgraded). Robert Weis, Annette's brother, stated that no one in the family knew he was under psychiatric care until informed by the FBI.

With Bishop disappeared from the Smoky Mountains, to who knows where, the investigators continued to focus on in the Washington area on Bishop's life and career, hoping to turn up valuable clues as to what happened and where he might be off to. Of course, all exit points from the country were under close surveillance, and agents fanned out all over the country to conduct interviews.

VI.

THE TRAIL GOES COLD

In August of 1976, five months after the Bishop family killings, in a bizarre action of bureaucracy the State Department formally fired William Bradford Bishop, Jr. It was the position of the Department that Bishop was alive, out of the country "on unauthorized leave." So, when there was no response to a registered letter sent to his home address ordering him back to work, he was officially terminated from the Department of State. Thus ended a productive and promising career of one of the smartest and most dedicated foreign service employees in quite a while.

As the months grew into years the Bishop case came up from time to time on various popular television shows, like *America's Most Wanted*, or *Unsolved Mysteries*. These shows never added anything new. They recapitulated the known facts of the case, showed Bishop family home movies to illustrate what a handsome and loving family they appeared to be, and sometimes featured various law enforcement and media types at a roundtable discussing the case. Some thought Bishop was dead, others did not. Some brought up possible CIA connections, others brushed such suggestions aside. They speculated on various possible motives, but could never come up with anything even remotely plausible. They were left scratching their heads in the dark. The public was even more baffled.

Bishop was passed over for a promotion that he was counting on. Did that make him go home and slaughter his family? Not likely.

He resented his mother trying to run the household. Reason to slaughter the family? No.

Bishop wanted another foreign posting, Annette did not. Reason to wipe out his family? No.

He had been seeing a psychiatrist, and had been prescribed a low level drug, Serax, for depression and possible alcoholism. This did not seem to affect him unduly, and was not a condition to cause him to kill his family.

Some kind of psychotic breakdown? No one could fathom such a thing resulting in the murders of a beautiful family.

And so on ...

Probably the most intense probing as to a possible motive in the Bishop case was conducted by the famous FBI profiler John Douglas, who devoted a portion of his book *The Anatomy of Motive* to Bishop. He and the FBI did a fugitive assessment on Bishop at Quantico, and updated it each year. They concluded that with his foreign service background, language abilities and general sophistication, Bishop could fit in anywhere in the world. But, it was felt that Europe would constitute the greatest comfort zone for Bishop. They studied his vacations, lifestyle and general habits in an attempt to determine what sorts of milieu he would be attracted to. And they attempted to project what his psychological state might be, and how he might be conducting himself. All this produced interesting information, but Bishop remained a fugitive. If he was alive. And there were those in the FBI, including Douglas, who wondered about that.

Douglas looked intensively into Bishop's life and career for clues as to what might have "set him off." As with other such investigations nothing very negative stood out—no major financial difficulties, no marital problems or girlfriends lurking in the background. On the contrary, almost everything turned up was extremely positive. Except for the psychiatrist visits, which even the State Department did not know about.

Douglas pondered the fact that Bishop had been passed over for a very much expected promotion to a much better position after having been kept for a rather long period of time in one position. Especially after his rather rapid rise prior to being reassigned to Washington. There was, Douglas knew, a certain precedent for middle-aged, professional men in a structured environment to suddenly crack when confronted with extreme frustration or disappointment. This could have been what happened to Bishop, though the extent and nature of the crime seemed extreme to the utmost.

Douglas noted that Bishop wasted no time in vacating the crime scene, and taking the evidence with him. The maps found in the car indicated, he thought, a certain degree of sophistication and planning. What he found highly unusual was the manner in which the family was killed, up close and personal, and very brutally. It was not "clean," like surprise gunshots to the back of the head. The Bishops were literally beaten to death—including a peaceful, sleeping five year old. The brutal killing of the three beautiful young boys bothered Douglas most painfully. As a parent himself, he found it almost impossible to imagine a father harming his sons in that way. He felt strongly that "it goes against all tenets of nature to imagine hurting your child, it is inconceivable to plan to brutally bludgeon him as he sleeps." But, he had run up against enough brutal and inconceivable crimes to know that they did happen. He felt that if Bishop did kill his family, as police believed, it had to be a completely willful act on his part. He had to be able to visualize what the end result of his actions would be—a chilling thought. And then, there was the disposal of the bodies, which shows more concern with destroying evidence than seeing to the dignity of the bodies and the eternal rest of the deceased.

Douglas kept coming back to focus on the murders themselves—the manner in which they were committed. To bludgeon one's family to death, there has to be some deep and very volatile anger, something hidden away, perhaps from the carefree demeanor of everyday life. Even if a person is a manic-depressive, and there is some evidence that Bishop was, you don't just suddenly, on the spur of the moment decide that things are really out of hand, go out and buy a hammer and some gasoline, and beat your family to death. There has to be some emotional buildup to it. So, in some form or another, Douglas believed that the notion of what he was going to do had to be brewing in Bishop's mind before the actual crime on March 1, 1976.

Douglas focused on trying to imagine what might have accounted for Bishop's evident rage and desperation. Was it the disappointment at being passed over for a promotion for the first time in his golden career? Depression? He was seeing a psychiatrist, who should have been able to detect warning signs. Tensions with his mother? A secret girlfriend? (In spite of the report of the woman in the sporting goods store in Jacksonville, North Carolina, holding the leash of Bishop's dog, there was no evidence of any extramarital affair.) Douglas could not conclude that any of those possibilities constituted any logical motive for crimes, certainly not for the brutal manner in which the murders were committed. The little string of possible motives were not internally consistent. Nothing seemed wrong with Bishop's life. Could not he have gotten divorced, resigned from the State Department, or just run off to Key West?

Douglas remained frustrated by the Bishop case. That in spite of how closely his life and career had been scrutinized, the man remained a mystery. There have been cases where persons are so consumed by their own self-image that their personal view of success and achievement is out of touch with reality. Douglas theorized that someone like Bishop would have great difficulty in admitting, to himself or others, that there might be anything wrong with him or his life. He could not see himself as anything less than "perfect," an image in itself out of touch with reality. When something unavoidability negative happens, like being passed over for a promotion that he implicitly believed he was entitled to, a person like Bishop, at the crisis point of middle age, might suddenly be consumed with the notion that things were not going to work out the way he had imagined, or dreamed. And, unable to stand the strain, exploded. Possible, Douglas thought. But far from convincing...

Douglas remained as frustrated as all the other investigators in believing that Bishop could not have accomplished his escape/disappearance completely on his own. He was seen in the company of the "dark skinned woman" holding the leash of his dog. His car was then abandoned hundreds of miles away in the mountains of Tennessee. How did he escape from that area? No one remembered any hitchhiker, or any man with a dog. He had to have had help! Who?

Douglas was asked to evaluate whether Bishop might kill again. How dangerous should he be considered? Here the pertinent elements seemed the same, if Bishop were a fugitive living in, say, Europe. If things were going well, reasonably his way, he could be mellow and content, charming even. But, if things took a wrong turn—watch out! Douglas felt that Bishop contained a very dangerous violent streak, one submerged most of the time, but there. Also, he felt that Bishop could be quite dangerous if faced with capture. Duly noted in the wanted bulletins and posters that went out all over the world.

Douglas indicated that he felt a degree of frustration with the Bishop case that was almost more than any other case he had studied.

He felt a tremendous need to understand—to know—what had gone on in the mind of William Bradford Bishop, Jr. before, during and after the killings of his family.

A theoretical psychological condition that might have applied to Bishop, and possibly explained his maniacal behavior, is something called "Catathymic Crisis," generally a term in forensic psychology. This theory was first presented by a Dr. Frederic Wertham in 1937 as a possible explanation for certain types of violent and seemingly motivation-less crimes. Dr. Wertham's theory describes a five stage process in which (1) a thinking disorder occurs within the mind of the criminal, (2) a plan is created to commit a violent criminal act, (3) internal emotional tension forces the commission of the criminal act, which leads to (4) a superficial calmness in which the need to commit the violent act is eliminated and normal activity can be conducted, and (5) the mind adjusts itself and understands that the thinking process that caused the commission of the criminal act was flawed and the mind makes adjustments in order to prevent further criminal activity.

Put a bit more simply, in layman's terms, "Catathymic Crisis" describes someone who kills a person or persons who they are very close to and still grieves for the victim(s) just as if he were innocent of any crime. Catathymic episodes start with anxiety and depression over emotionally tense relationships and end up with the belief that the only way out is murder.

If any of this applied to Bishop, even slightly, then his psychological state would have been far more serious and critical than anyone, his psychiatrist included, perceived.

In 1977, in what many considered an appalling exercise in poor taste two young men, Steve Latske and Stephen Deady, composed what they thought was a creative venture— "The Ballad of Bradford Bishop." Inexplicably, it was recorded by Adelphi Records and got a fair amount of play on Country and Western stations in the Washington,

D.C., region. It is instructive, perhaps, of a certain mindset, to present here some printed verses from "The Ballad of Bradford Bishop."

IT BEGAN IN BETHESDA ON A COLD WINTER'S DAY,
BRAD BISHOP WAS WASTED, HIS MIND GONE ASTRAY.
HE SAID WHAT I THINK I NEED IS A LONG HOLIDAY
SO HE PICKED UP HIS FAMILY AND TOOK THEM AWAY.

BRADFORD BISHOP, TIRED OF TAKING THEIR GUFF,
BRADFORD BISHOP GOT A POKER AND SHOWED
    THEM HIS STUFF.
FOR HE'S NINE YEARS PAST 30, A MOST DESPERATE MAN.
KILLED HIS WHOLE FAMILY, TOOK OFF AND RAN.

INTO NORTH CAROLINA, THE DRIVE TOOK ALL NIGHT.
THE KILLINGS WENT SMOOTHLY, THE TIMING JUST
    RIGHT.
FIVE BATTERED BODIES, A HORRIBLE SIGHT.
HE PUT 'EM IN DITCHES AND PACKED THE DIRT TIGHT.

AT THE DEPARTMENT OF STATE HE WAS ONLY A PAWN,
HIS CHANCES WERE FADING, HIS HOPES WERE ALL GONE.
HIS HOUSEHOLD WAS RUN BY HIS MOM'S IRON HAND.
BRADFORD WAS NEVER A FAMILY MAN.

NOW BRADFORD HAS GONE TO A DISTANT SHORE,
HE'S LEFT US BEHIND HIM, HE'LL MURDER NO MORE.
BUT THERE'S A LITTLE BRAD BISHOP IN ME AND IN YOU.
FOR A MAN ONLY DOES WHAT HE KNOWS HE CAN DO.

SOME DAY THEY'LL FIND HIM, DOWN IN OLD MEXICO,
WITH LEO HIS RETRIEVER, DRINKING JOSE CUERVO.
WHY DID HE DO IT, NO ONE CAN TELL.
HE TRADED HIS FAMILY FOR A TICKET TO HELL.

Someone else, it was believed, was preparing a movie script on the killings and subsequent disappearance of Bradford Bishop. Fortunately, no such film ever appeared. One can only imagine what sort of cinematic achievement such an effort might have been.

The TV programs produced a flurry of sightings all over the United States, and even Europe. Each one was investigated, but all proved to be of little value or significance. Until…

VII.

WHO WAS BRAD BISHOP?

The notion that Bishop was, or had been, some sort of spy persisted. Friends of the missing foreign service officer recalled that he told them of intelligence work in the army and "very sensitive assignments in the State Department."

Laurence Long, a Yale roommate and a Bethesda neighbor said Bishop told him how, as an Army intelligence operative, he was assigned to spy on an Eastern European (it was Yugoslav) ski team appearing at a meet in Italy. Another former Yale roommate, New York businessman Stephen Wilson, recalled that Bishop had told him that he was "in Army intelligence, it was the thing to do, where the action was, and besides it was good duty."

Wilson and Long also talked to a third former roommate who said that around 1964 Bishop had called him at a bank in New York where he worked and said that he had used him as a reference for "a very sensitive position" he was seeking with the State Department. The banker, who would not talk about that incident with a reporter, told Wilson and Long that he subsequently received a letter from the State Department thanking him for "very candid" answers about Bishop.

When the banker saw Bishop about three years later and asked him about the job, Bishop told him, "I can't talk about it..."

When told of such speculations by Bishop's former roommates and friends, Annette Bishop's brother, Robert Weis, said that "the thought has crossed our minds that Bishop was, or is, a spy."

State Department officials insisted that Bishop was nothing more than what he appeared to be, a middle level bureaucrat working with foreign trade. Montgomery County investigators said that such speculation was beyond the purview of the investigation. One policeman commented, about Bishop possibly being a spy, "But even if he is, how does that help us solve this thing?"

When a sophomore and junior at Yale, Bishop spent two years in Calhoun College in a group of rooms dubbed "The Presidential Suite" by fellow students because the young men living there were a Lincoln, Wilson, Polk and Franklin Pierce. When he heard about the Bishop killings, Wilson began telephoning the other ex-residents of the suite. He said they had reached a consensus that possible involvement in intelligence activities might explain away "the preposterous notion that Brad could have done this." The banker, Wilson said, remains convinced that Brad is, or was, "an agent or spy for the CIA."

George Hefferan, a Portland, Maine, lawyer who was one of the roommates said that back in 1962 he had spent a week in Monterey visiting with the Bishops. "We didn't talk about it," he said, "but I knew that he was studying Serbo-Croatian, and I assumed that everyone there was in intelligence work. What he went on to do, I can't say."

Former roommate and Bethesda neighbor Long said, "Brad was never real specific about just what he did at State. He was supposedly specializing with some sort of trade group, but I know that I have suspicions about that. And, he was always making these mysterious trips that he never talked about."

A State Department official said that a large part of Bishop's duties was to represent the United States government at international trade agreement meetings at Geneva, Switzerland, and elsewhere. Although Bishop held a top secret clearance, officials indicated that is what every foreign service officer must have, hence sensitive background checks.

As months passed after the disappearance of Bishop, and without the surfacing of any meaningful clues, and most importantly the absence of any motive that could drive a man to such horrific crimes, the police and newspapers continued to gather information on Bishop. *The Washington Post* published an account of Bishop, his life, family and career that was particularly detailed. It is presented here because it puts perhaps the whole thing in some sort of perspective:

> *The romance of Annette Weis and Bradford Bishop began in California. Annette was born in Toledo, Ohio, on April 14, 1938. Her parents, Gilbert and Eunice Weis, moved to California when she and her brother, Robert, were children. The family settled in the Los Angeles suburb of San Marino, and Annette attended nearby South Pasadena high school.*
>
> *It was there that she met Brad Bishop, the only child of Lobelia Amaryllis and William Bradford Bishop, an independent geologist, who lived in South Pasadena, the Los Angeles suburb where Brad was born August 1, 1936.*
>
> *Brad graduated from high school in 1954, the year before Annette did, and he went east to study economics at Yale. But the miles did not diminish their romance.*
>
> *At Yale, Bishop was remembered as an above-average student academically. He played freshman football, talked about being a doctor, and was very gregarious.*
>
> *One of his roommates, who went home with him for a short visit, recalled that Bishop's father was "a quiet man by comparison to his mother, who was like Brad, very outgoing personality," which the friend attributed to her French background.*

On the same trip the roommate met Annette and was impressed by her as "a lovely girl, and bright, too."

Bishop would have graduated with the class of 1958 at Yale. But he dropped out just before the start of his senior year. One friend thought it had something to do with a shortage of money in the house— "his father was always complaining about how the big oil companies were rough on a private geologist." Brad took a job "digging ditches." When he returned to Yale with the class of 1959, he had given up plans to become a physician.

Shortly after he graduated from Yale in 1959, Brad and Annette were married in San Clemente, California, where her family had moved, and where her parents still live.

Brad enlisted in the Army on August 5, 1959, at Fort Dix, New Jersey. After basic training at Fort Benning he enrolled in the student battalion of the Army Intelligence School at Fort Holabird, in Baltimore.

Bishop finished intelligence school in the summer of 1960, and immediately was sent to the Army's language school in Monterey, California, where he learned the Serbo-Croatian language.

While the Bishops were living in Monterey, their first son, William Bradford Bishop, III, was born on August 14, 1961. Just 10 days after his son was born, Bishop was assigned to the 163rd military intelligence battalion in Europe, where his wife and young son soon joined him. For the next two years Bishop served in Europe, primarily in Italy where he carried out mundane spying efforts such as listening to Yugoslav radio broadcasts and translating Serbo-Croatian journals into English.

When his four-year enlistment ended on August 14, 1963, Staff Sergeant Bishop accepted an honorable discharge in Verona, Italy. The only medal he showed for four years and eight days of military service was for good conduct. The Bishops stayed on in

Italy, and Bishop enrolled at the Florence campus of Middlebury (VT) College, where he studied Italian.

The family returned to the United States in the spring of 1964, and Bishop obtained a master's degree in Italian from the main Middlebury campus in Vermont. That summer the Bishops returned to California, where on July 30, their second son, Brenton Germain Bishop, was born, in Pasadena.

In the fall of 1965 Bishop came to Washington and, armed with a master's degree and fluency in two foreign languages, he entered the State Department's foreign service program. At 29, Bishop was the oldest member of the group of 30 candidates who attended an eight week orientation course, then held at the Foreign Service Institute's old headquarters at the Arlington Towers.

"Because of his age and languages, Brad entered at the highest level for foreign service officers," one classmate recalled. By November Bishop had been promoted to foreign service officer grade 7. "Brad was intellectually superior, clearly one of the brightest guys in the class," said another classmate.

Shortly before Christmas Bishop got his first overseas assignment, as a junior officer in the embassy at Addis Ababa, Ethiopia. A woman who was then a teenager in the American compound in Addis Ababa recalls looking up to the Bishops "as really the ideal family. He was smart and handsome and she was her own person—a mother and a wife, and also into art." Bishop was named a consular officer in January 1967, and promoted to FSO 6 that June. In January 1968 he was transferred to Milan, Italy, where his fluency in Italian helped advance his career. His next promotion, to FSO 5, came in Italy in May 1969.

The Bishops were back in the U.S. in 1970, as is customary in the foreign service, and Bishop was back to school—this time to the University of California, Los Angeles (UCLA). He studied there throughout the summer and fall, graduating with all A's in the spring of 1971, with a second master's degree, in African studies. The Bishops lived in their hometown of South Pasadena during that time, so Annette and the boys were able to spend considerable time with her parents, and on February 12, 1971, their third, and last, son, Geoffrey Corder Bishop, was born in Pasadena.

Bishop returned to Washington and the State Department in June 1971, and was assigned to the East African office in the Bureau of African Affairs. When the Bishops moved back to Washington that summer, they were accompanied by his mother, who, following the death of her husband, had sold the house in South Pasadena. When Brad was posted for his next foreign assignment, to Gaborone, Botswana, in January 1972, it was a family of six—husband, wife, mother and three sons—who made the trip. In Botswana Bishop was deputy chief of the mission, a position that made him second only to the ambassador. He had been promoted to FSO 4 after receiving his second master's degree, and one of his FSI classmates—who keeps close tabs on such matters—noted that "Brad was the first one in the class to make it to grade 4."

Persons who knew the Bishops in either Ethiopia or Botswana, or who had friends who did, noticed a slight change in the family on the second trip to Africa. "Annette wasn't as anxious to play the loyal State Department wife bit," said one friend. "She didn't always jump in and volunteer to bake cookies or help with the constant round of dinner parties." The change might have been attributed to the presence of Bishop's mother, an active, younger looking woman who was anxious to take on her share of responsibilities in the family. Mrs. Bishop, Sr., as Lobelia was known, took over part of the household duties, and especially liked to play with the baby, Geoff.

The Bishops returned to Washington in 1974 and settled into the modern frame house at 8103 Lily Stone Drive in the Carderock Springs section of Bethesda. Bishop was given one of those nondescript interim assignments that foreign service officers accept as part of the territory. His title was Assistant of the Special Trade Activities and Commercial Treaties Division in the Office of International Trade of the Bureau of Economic and Business Affairs.

Bishop's associates at State scoffed at the suggestion, made by some of Bishop's roommates at Yale, that Bishop could have been a spy within the State Department. "That was a totally stupid story," one man said. He added that Bishop was "relatively content" in his current post, which permitted him considerable overseas travel. "He was a great family man. I ran into him in Geneva in December and he showed me a postcard one of his boys had sent him. My kids love me, too, but State Department kids don't send postcards every time their father takes a trip. He had some special relationship."

The Bishops' neighborhood in Bethesda is filled with upwardly mobile families, including several other State Department foreign service families. The Bishops fitted in beautifully. They joined the Carderock Tennis and Swim Club, where the older boys swam competitively and Brad and Annette were popular tennis partners.

And again, because, according to some neighbors, the senior Mrs. Bishop "acted like the mother of the family," Annette was free to pursue her interest in art. Having attended the University of California at Berkeley while Brad was at Yale, she now enrolled as a full time student at the main campus of the University of Maryland at College Park.

To the above account of Bishop and his career must be added these extraordinary laudatory comments on Bishop and his family from friends and colleagues, taken from other news articles. The term most commonly used is "attractive." It will be noted that Ambassador Korry, who at first claimed to only barely remember Bishop, had a sudden resuscitation of his memory and recalled Bishop clearly with the highest compliments.

"He was Mr. Clean, an All-American boy," said Jack Gloster, a former associate of Bishop in the State Department. "They were a very attractive couple." The children, said Gloster, were "almost stereotyped foreign service kids"—pleasant, active, polite.

"He was a first class young foreign service officer whom I pushed along as fast as I could," said Edward Korry, U.S. Ambassador to Ethiopia when Bishop was stationed there. "He was a good looking man, eager to do whatever he could," Korry said. "His wife was among the loveliest of the American mission wives."

Eugene Rosenfeld, director of the United States Information Service in Ethiopia, said Bishop, was "a very attractive guy" and that his wife, Annette, was "extremely attractive." Another associate from Ethiopia said the Bishops were "perhaps the most popular couple in Addis Ababa."

Rosenfeld, the former head of USIS in Addis Ababa, recalled that Bishop was "very hard working" when he knew him there and that he was "tall and athletic." Rosenfeld added, "He was an amateur actor and played in a production we put on in Addis Ababa." He remembered Annette Bishop as "a vivacious and intelligent woman."

Charles Rudd, a former neighbor who now lives in Gaithersburg, Maryland, said of the Bishop family, "They were the kind of people—it's a typical thing—you wouldn't think anyone would want to hurt them."

VIII.

QUESTIONS

There are many disturbing questions in the Bishop case. Unanswered questions. Perhaps unanswerable questions. But, they are vitally important and must be asked. If there are no answers, the subjects must still be thought about, pondered, explored, in the hope that some further insight will emerge. It is not a simple process. It is very challenging. In this chapter I will go through the case chronologically, from the morning of the murders to the last "sighting," asking questions where they need to be asked. If there is a possible answer I will suggest such. Where there is no answer, I will so indicate and leave the matter to speculation, if that be possible. I think that we will see, when all the questions have been addressed that things do not quite add up, that they have not been as straight forward or as simple as some have suggested.

We are informed that on the morning of 1 March 1976 William Bradford Bishop, Jr. learned that he had been passed over by the State Department for a promotion. A promotion that he felt was much over-due and very much deserved. He had risen rapidly in the State Department, the first of his class to reach the grade of F-4. But then his career had sort of stalled. Returning from a diplomatic post in Milan,

Italy, to Washington he was placed in a rather routine bureaucratic desk job. And had stayed in that position rather too long, he thought. He wanted another overseas posting. His wife and mother did not. At the very least he thought he deserved to be promoted to F-3, with more money, prestige and future possibilities. Then suddenly, almost out of nowhere, this was not to be.

There must have been something very negative that came up to so affect Bishop's career. Perhaps there was even some sort of signal that his State Department career might be coming to an end. It had to be something in Bishop's past, something that probably he knew about and perhaps had tried to keep hidden. Or was assured that would be kept hidden. We don't know. Were there outside forces "guiding" this negativity? Did someone have some sort of hold over Bishop that could have very negatively affected his career, his value to the State Department? We don't know. But it could be possible.

All we know is that Bishop was terribly disappointed, upset, angry even. He told his secretary that afternoon that he "did not feel well, might be coming down with the flu." And left "early"—5:30 p.m.

What was Bishop wearing that day at his office at Foggy Bottom? The 1970s were still a rather formal time, more so in the State Department. So we can assume that he was probably wearing a conservative suit and tie, dark in color. Why do we ask this detail? Because it might have some bearing on a matter raised later.

We are told that Bishop drove from his place of employment to a suburban shopping center in Maryland, the Montgomery Mall, not far from his house. And there purchased at a Sears store with his Bank of America credit card a short handled, four pound "sledge hammer," and a two and one half gallon gas can. He then withdrew $400 from a savings account, and filled his brown Chevy station wagon and the gas can with gas at a nearby gas station using a gas company card (found later).

We must ask why he made these purchases. Was it "spur of the moment," or something he had been thinking about for a long time?

And why use a credit card if one is planning a crime that one intends to get away with? There is a certain lack of stealth here, a certain pattern of behavior that is not quite explainable. Could something have been influencing Bishop, something connected with his failure to achieve the expected job promotion? We don't know, but wonder if there might be some sort of connection.

We know that Bishop was at his home by 6:30 p.m., because a neighbor saw him outside the house at that time. Did he leave the Sears purchases in the rear of the station wagon? Probably. And then went into the house and greeted his mother, wife and three sons. In what must have been a sort of family ritual, the father coming home from the office. Did Bishop change from the suit? Or just perhaps remove the jacket and tie?

We must imagine that some sort of effort "to get comfortable" was engaged in. And did he get a beer and settle in front of the TV, perhaps watching the evening news or a basketball game while waiting for dinner to be served? One imagines that the Bishop family ate at a dinner table, and talked of the day's events. Like any other family. Did Bishop mention the fact of being passed over for the expected promotion? We don't know. And what about after dinner? Did Bishop watch some more TV? What sorts of thoughts were going through his head? We don't—cannot—know. But he must have had what followed later that night very much on his mind. He would have to. It would be most abnormal not to. But then that was not to be a normal night...

Now we come to the killings, where there are, in my opinion, a number of rather serious discrepancies. The authorities established that the killings were initiated at about 11 p.m. How could they determine that? We shall see.

It was believed that the killer, assumed to be Bishop, attacked his wife first, as she was reading in the first floor level den near the entryway of the front door. The killer must have approached her from behind and struck one or more blows to her head, just below the right ear with a heavy blunt object, believed to be the short-handled sledge hammer. And then, according to investigators, no sooner had the killer accomplished this first homicide, when he was surprised and startled to hear the mother, Lobelia, entering the house from being out walking the dog, Leo. This was a nightly routine at 11 p.m. according to neighbors (hence the time of the killings). Here we must ask a very important question. Why did Bishop initiate the killing of his wife, so near to the front door, when he knew his mother was walking the dog and would return at any minute? This makes no sense. Could he have forgotten his mother's routine? Very unlikely. And why did he not wait until the whole family was asleep?

The killer tried hastily to conceal Annette Bishop's body with one or two coats (where were they retrieved from?), but Lobelia Bishop, on entering the house, realized immediately that something was most terribly wrong. Did she confront a crazed individual holding a bloody hammer? Or was her reaction more instinctual? Whatever—we are told that she dropped the dog's leash and dashed up the stairs, and locked herself in the bathroom at the top of the stairs. The killer quickly followed and proceeded to kick in the bathroom door. We have seen on a TV program a photograph of the splintered, hollow core door obviously kicked in at the bottom. What is interesting is that the lock mechanism of almost all hollow core doors is rather weak. The easiest way to disable such a locked door is with one good strong kick against the portion of the door next to or on the locked part. Or, with a four pound hammer one or more heavy blows on the knob. Kicking in the bottom, where the door would be most resilient is not the most effective approach. In this case the result was the same. The door was broken open and the killer rushed in and proceeded to beat Lobelia Bishop to death. That is what the police said. And then, according to investigators, the killer entered the first upstairs bedroom, where one boy was sleeping alone and killed him with one or more blows to the head. In the second bedroom the two other sleeping boys were said to have been killed in the same manner. A TV show displayed pictures of bloodstained pillows where the boys' heads had rested.

The problem with this reconstruction is that there is almost no likelihood that the killings could have happened in this order. First, breaking down the door and beating Lobelia to death in the bathroom must have created an ungodly racket. The boys would have been awakened, possibly have gotten out of bed in fear. The boys would have to have been killed as they were sleeping. Could the killer have killed Annette Bishop downstairs, then gone upstairs, killed the boys and returned to the first floor—aware the Lobelia Bishop would be returning shortly from walking the dog? Did he plan to ambush her as she entered the house? We don't know. We just have to think about all this and the questions that are raised about the sequence of the killings, and why they were initiated when and how they were. Again, things are not adding up. Could there have been someone else involved? Someone who did not know that Lobelia Bishop would be out of the house?

After the killings the bodies were wrapped in blankets and removed to the station wagon backed up to the stone walkway leading from the front door. One would presume carried, but some reports indicate bloody drag marks across some portions of the floors. Why would Bishop drag the bodies? He was certainly strong enough to carry only one of them with ease. Dragging shows a certain disrespect and insensitivity, to say nothing of brutality.

It must be noted that the murder weapon, presumed to be the short handled sledge hammer purchased earlier that day, was never found. Presumably it was carried from the house and disposed of somewhere between there and North Carolina, either by throwing it out the window of the vehicle, or while stopped at a rest stop the killer threw it into bushes, or perhaps into a body of water.

Then we have the almost 300 mile drive through the night to an incredibly remote and out of the way spot in eastern North Carolina. Could he have made the trip on one tank of gas? Conceivably. But he had to pass through several toll booths. Why on earth did the killer pick that particular spot on a sandy logging road just south of Columbia, North Carolina? If, conceivably, Bishop had been at a CIA training facility at Harvey's Point across Albemarle Sound, he just might have been slightly familiar with that remote spot. But why drive all that way, leaving behind a house that was quite obviously the scene of a crime? It makes no sense.

And then we have the crude and rather unfinished manner in which the bodies were disposed of. A shallow grave, very shallow, with the bodies crudely arranged, and then some gasoline sprinkled, hardly enough to create "a funeral pyre." The whole episode speaks of extreme lack of feeling and respect, almost as if the person disposing of the bodies was someone other than Bishop who just wanted to "get it over with and get out." Or perhaps that was his out of mind state at the time? We cannot know.

What of the gas can and the tools left behind? A shovel and a pitchfork. The shovel we can understand, but a pitchfork? That does not seem likely. Such an implement is not much used in suburban gardening. In fact, it would be more likely used in a rather rustic farm, such as might be found, say, in Eastern Europe or some such place. We have a hard time envisioning the implement's usefulness in transporting or burying bodies. It just seems strange.

One of two prime pieces of evidence—in fact seemingly the only physical evidence—was "one good fingerprint belonging to Bishop" lifted from the gas can. The man had bought the can, of course his prints would be on it. But might there be other implications? We shall see...

There is no mention of any prints on the tools. Had they been wiped clean? If so, why? We have no answer.

The long drive through the night with the bodies—and evidently with Leo, the dog, who was not found at the house or anywhere around—seems very strange. As does the crude partial burying and burning of the bodies. All of it defies any sort of rational explanation. Investigators assumed that Bishop was attempting to cover up or conceal the crime, planning to make some sort of getaway. If so, he was certainly going about all of it in a very strange and disorganized manner. He might have guessed that the family would not be missed from the house for a matter of days, and might have thought that no one would come upon the bodies in the piney woods—and probably did. That is what we assume was his thinking. But we do not really know what was going on in the mind of Bradford Bishop. Or if he was thinking at all…

Now we come to what may be the most bizarre episode in this whole sad and sorry story. And that is the appearance of Bradford Bishop at a sporting goods store in Jacksonville, North Carolina, a medium sized town some 100 miles southeast of the spot where the bodies were discovered. Jacksonville, a small port for fishing vessels, and surrounded to the south and east by the large Marine Corps installation Camp Lejeune, could not be considered exactly on the route to any specific place, over secondary and indirect roads, unless it might be Wilmington, North Carolina, farther down the coast. It was late the same afternoon when Bishop entered the sporting goods store and made a purchase of items totaling $15.60. What these items were is unknown, but the proprietor of the store thought they might be something like socks and a sweatshirt. What is interesting is that Bishop used his Bank of America credit card. His signature was verified by FBI experts, so indicating to authorities the last time that Bishop can be proven to be alive.

What is further of great interest is that this proprietor described Bishop, definitely remembering him when shown a photograph, as being very normal acting, polite and well spoken. And dressed in a suit! The proprietor commented on that because it was so unusual for his customers. And, he mentioned the "Caribbean looking woman" waiting outside with what appeared to be Leo, the Bishop's Golden Retriever, on a leash. The proprietor mentioned that he definitely thought Bishop and the woman were together, as in a couple.

Taking the most obvious question—why would Bishop be dressed in a suit? There may be several theories, but we will get to those later. But, off hand it would seem most incongruous. And, normal-acting, polite and well-spoken? Rather strange for a man who had just killed his entire family, attempted to bury and burn their bodies, and was fleeing. Very odd. Why did he use his credit card, when he had just committed such a monumental crime? And, why was he in Jacksonville, North Carolina? Was the fact it was a sort of port an issue? Or the proximity of Camp Lejeune? We don't know. Or perhaps he was on his way to Wilmington, farther south. And the woman? Who could she have possibly been? And involved in what way with Bishop? We may have some ideas about that, but they will have to wait.

It was ten days later that the station wagon was discovered abandoned at the western edge of Great Smoky Mountain National Park. We have to wonder, why that rather remote location? And, the items in the car? A shotgun and box of shells. What possibly for? Why abandon these? And the two coats and the suitcase full of men's clothing and toiletries? Why were these taken and then left? Makes no sense. Unless there was some other plan afoot, that suddenly perhaps took precedence. The park area was thoroughly searched but other than some scent trails that the dogs were able to follow there was no sign of Bishop, no indication of how he might have left the park area except that perhaps someone picked him up. The woman? Possibly. But, again, we have to ask what sort of role could she have possibly been playing? Taking off with a brutal murderer of his family. Not very romantic. Was something else going on? Was she an agent of some entity? We will get back to that possibility.

After the Great Smoky disappearance there was no solid information on Bishop's location until the sightings in Sweden and in Italy. In both of these cases the individuals reporting the sightings told what they saw—or what they thought they saw. Investigators were somewhat dubious about both of those sightings, but of course they had to follow up on them with the full force of the resources available. After all, Bradford Bishop was one of the world's most wanted fugitives. The matter of the third sighting seems quite a bit more serious and authoritative, given the nature of the persons making the report. But, again, nothing led to any apprehension of Bishop. One has to wonder? I will return to this third sighting later, because there are some interesting and disturbing ramifications in this incident.

Later on I am going to raise a very direct series of questions and deal with them as might be the case in a court of law, an exercise in imagination, if you will. We shall see ... As I was pondering these questions that came up in the Bishop case, I decided to make another call to Detective Cady at the Montgomery County Sheriff's Department, to see if anything new and interesting had come up.

IX.

SOME "SIGHTINGS"
AND A MYSTERIOUS LETTER

In January, 1979, a Swedish woman who claimed to be a family friend of William Bradford Bishop, Jr., told police in Stockholm that she had seen Bishop on the streets of that city on two separate occasions the previous July. The woman's report prompted a six month investigation by Swedish police, and by the FBI, which sent an agent to Stockholm to assist in the investigation and search. Although there had been numerous reports of sightings of Bishop in the three years since he disappeared, one police official stated, "This is the first solid one."

The woman, whose identity was withheld by the authorities, stated that she "knew Bishop well when he served with the State Department in Africa" in the mid 1960s, according to a statement released by the FBI field office in Baltimore. In that statement the woman was said to have told police that Bishop was wearing a beard.

Major Wayne G. Brown of the Montgomery County Police Department issued a statement that was unlike dozens of previous reports of sightings of Bishop and his possible whereabouts: "This apparently is a good sighting." The statement went on to say that the FBI was taking the woman's story "very seriously." But, the official FBI statement added that "the individual making the report of the sightings was not was in a position to be sure Bishop was spotted." It went on to say that "Swedish police are cooperating with the FBI and the U.S. Embassy in Stockholm in efforts to locate and possibly identify the subject."

Since Bishop's disappearance authorities had checked out hundreds of reports that Bishop had been seen all throughout America, and in Africa and Europe. The reason the latest tip from Sweden was being taken so seriously was that it was the first to come from someone who had been a friend of Bishop and his family.

An FBI spokesman in Baltimore said that agents from the FBI European staff had been conferring closely with Swedish national police for some time. The most recent meeting was said to have in early January, 1979, in Stockholm with an agent from the FBI London office.

Gary Reals, a reporter for Swedish radio station WMAL said from Stockholm that the woman who made the reports was a Swedish national who was living in Addis Ababa, Ethiopia, when Bishop was stationed there in the mid-1960s. Reals reported that Swedish police had been conducting a covert investigation for the last six months, but were resisting pleas by American officials to distribute a photograph of Bishop to the news media in Sweden. The sightings occurred during the first week of July, 1978, according to the FBI.

Major Brown, whose department turned the search for Bishop over to the FBI after murder indictments were returned against him, said that no one from the Montgomery County Police or Sheriff's Department would go to Sweden "because the FBI has jurisdiction under an unlawful flight warrant."

The name of the woman who reported sighting Bishop was not released. Reals said that she was believed to have been a close friend of the Bishop family during their stay in Ethiopia. He went on to state that the woman was either an employee, or married to an employee, of the Swedish Embassy in Addis Ababa at the time, or was possibly married to an Ethiopian diplomat.

Several American diplomats who were stationed in Ethiopia with Bishop told investigators that they could not recall any Swedish woman, but one added, "The Bishops were a very gregarious family who entertained all sorts of people in their home."

The result of this very intensive six-month investigation was an announcement in January 1979 by police in Stockholm that "there was no reason to believe that William Bradford Bishop, Jr., was still in Sweden." There was no comment on whether he had actually ever been in Sweden. Gunnar Larsson of the Interpol section of the Swedish national police said no new leads had been developed in the six months since a woman reported that she saw Bishop in a downtown park on two occasions the previous July. Swedish police refused to reveal the identity of the woman because she told them that she was afraid of Bishop, whom she said she knew when they were both living in Addis Ababa, Ethiopia, in the mid-1960s.

Swedish police stated that the woman came to them on July 4, 1978, stating that she had passed within six feet of Bishop while walking in Kungsträdgården, the main park in central Stockholm. She added that she had seen the same man from 30 to 35 feet away from the same man three days earlier in the same park, which is a popular gathering place for the residents of Stockholm. The woman, who was believed to have been connected to the Swedish Embassy in Ethiopia when Bishop was assigned to the U.S. Embassy there, said that Bishop had grown a full beard.

Gary Reals, who broke the story in Stockholm, reported from the Swedish capital that the same woman had gone to the police about Bishop in November 1977. Reals quoted a Swedish police officer as saying the woman reported receiving word from a mutual friend that Bishop might be coming to Sweden. The Swedish public learned of that story for the first time on January 5, 1979.

Contrary to an earlier report that Swedish police opposed an FBI request to publicize the manhunt in Sweden, Lars Jilmstad, information officer for the national police force, said that the drawback of enlisting the aid of the public was with the news media. Ronnie Olsson, acting news director of *Aftonbladat*, an afternoon tabloid that ran the story on its front page, confirmed that the paper's normal policy bans printing photographs of criminal suspects. "We run pictures only after a conviction," he said.

Police in Sweden complain that radio stations will not broadcast the license plate number of a getaway vehicle, saying that to do so would "constitute an invasion of privacy."

Jilmstad stated that Bishop's photograph and description had been sent to every police station in the country, and every detail of the crime and all ramifications had been incorporated into the national police nationwide computer network. The belief that Bishop was no longer in Sweden, if he had ever been, came from the experience of the Swedish police that criminals, like other citizens, eventually get ensnared in bureaucratic red tape in a country where buying a television set or renting an apartment requires extensive proof of identity. Swedish police also pointed out that it would be relatively easy to move in and out of the country because no passports are required of Scandinavians to travel between Sweden, Norway, Finland and Denmark. Swedish would have been an easy language for Bishop to pick up, given his facility for language.

Throughout the hunt for Bishop the FBI, working with the State Department, contacted a number of Americans living overseas who had known the Bishops during their various foreign assignments. But, a knowledgeable source in Stockholm said that no one in Sweden had been notified under the FBI program, and that a Swedish woman "definitely was not among anyone anywhere who was contacted."

Of all the various reported sightings, the one in Sweden was the first to be taken very seriously, according to all authorities.

There was a possible third sighting of Bishop in Sweden when it was reported that a Stockholm policeman may have seen him on a Stockholm street shortly after the alleged friend of the Bishop family reported seeing Bishop twice in a Stockholm park. But because the Swedish police did not get a photograph of Bishop from the FBI until about a month after the alleged July sightings in the park, the officer could not positively identify Bishop. Although the policeman was aware that Bishop was being sought in the city, he had only a written physical description to go on. A spokesman for the U.S. Embassy in Stockholm said that Bishop's photograph was turned over to Swedish authorities in August, 1978. The woman reported seeing a "bearded Bishop" in the city park on July 1 and 4.

The possible third sighting of Bishop in Sweden was reported to the chief of Stockholm's criminal investigation bureau when he distributed Bishop's photograph to his detectives and one of them said that he might have seen the suspect on a city street sometime in mid-July, according to Ben Schaumburg, the security officer at the American Embassy in Stockholm.

There was a flurry of excitement with these sightings, prompted by the FBI request in January 1979 that the Swedish authorities enlist the aid of Stockholm residents in looking for Bishop. But police said that since the previous summer the trail had gone cold. Inspector Gunnar Larsson of the Interpol office of the Swedish police stated, "We did everything to locate him, from the July sightings until September. At that time, when we had turned up absolutely no further reports or even clues, we have done nothing much until this recent FBI request of citizen aid."

Larsson commented that the woman who reported the initial sightings told Swedish police that she had known the Bishops when she had worked in the Swedish Embassy in Addis Ababa, Ethiopia, in the mid-1960s when Bishop was assigned to the U.S. Embassy there. She said that she was "a frequent visitor to the Bishop home," and described herself as "the best friend" of Bishop's wife, Annette.

The woman's identity had been kept secret because she feared Bishop and knew that "she could be a very important witness" in the worldwide search for him, Larsson said. He added that the woman was in her 40s or 50s, and was married to an Ethiopian at the time she lived in Addis Ababa. She later returned to Stockholm and resigned from the Swedish Ministry, and gained employment until January 1979 with a private firm in Stockholm. Larsson stated that the woman first came to Swedish police in November 1977, to report that the international fugitive Bishop might attempt to take refuge in Sweden "because he knew so many Swedes." She said she came to this conclusion, and decided to report it, after she and other Swedish friends who had been mutual friends of the Bishops "had been discussing his terrible crime and had speculated on where Bishop might go if he were alive." She said that they had agreed that Sweden and Australia were among the mostly likely placed he might try to hide.

Larsson said he sent a detective to the woman's apartment to interview her, "but there was not much we could do to allay her fears." He said that Swedish police were already well aware that Bishop was a fugitive from the crime(s) of murder in the United States and that there was an international warrant out for him.

The Swedish Interpol inspector did comment that he and other Swedish authorities were somewhat skeptical of the woman's report, noting that she had not seen Bishop in ten years, and that the man she saw and thought was Bishop was wearing a beard. The inspector mused that "the best theory in this case is that Bishop committed suicide and was eaten by bears in the Smoky Mountains."

After the trail had gone completely cold in Sweden in January 1979, there was no further commentary on Bishop until in June of 1979. The Baltimore office of the FBI, out of which the search of Bishop had been coordinated, reported that Bishop might have been seen in Italy five months earlier, (January 1979). FBI officials reported that agents had interviewed a State Department employee who reported seeing Bishop on January 11 in the southern Italian resort town of Sorrento. At that time European and American newspapers were carrying prominent reports that Bishop had been sighted twice in Stockholm, Sweden, in July 1978. The Baltimore FBI office said that agents were working closely with Italian authorities to determine the validity of the latest alleged sighting. The report was considered plausible because Bishop spoke very fluent Italian, having lived in Italy on three different occasions—in Verona from 1961 to 1963 as an agent of U.S. Army Intelligence, in Florence as a graduate student in 1963 and 1964, and in Milan as a diplomatic envoy in 1968 and 1969.

Details of the latest Bishop sighting were made available by Gary Reals, the reporter for Swedish radio station WMAL, who had covered the Bishop "sightings" closely in Stockholm. Reals stated that the man who allegedly sighted Bishop in Sorrento had been a co-worker with him both at the State Department and abroad, and had seen Bishop in Washington D.C. in February 1976, two weeks before the killings.

The witness, who was assigned to a U.S. diplomatic post in Africa, was vacationing in Sorrento according to Reals. This witness was using a public restroom in a large square in Sorrento when a bearded, bedraggled man walked in. The witness immediately recognized the man as Bishop. He said that he called out loudly, "Bradford Bishop!" or "You're Bradford Bishop!" Reals said. The bearded man then fled outside and disappeared into a blinding rainstorm.

The appearance of the bearded man spotted in Sorrento was a marked contrast to that of a man, also bearded, who was allegedly seen in a park in the capital city of Sweden six months earlier. The woman who identified the man in the park as Bishop described him as "nicely dressed, neat and well groomed."

The description of the bearded, disheveled man in the public restroom in Sorrento, had him with an unkempt beard, wearing dirty clothing, and looked like a bum or tramp, Reals reported.

Agents in Baltimore stated that they had known about the Sorrento "sighting" for some months, and that intensive coordinated investigations with Italian authorities had turned up no new clues. Another "trail" gone cold, evidently.

As these "sightings" were circulating in the press, Robert Weis, Annette Bishop's brother in Southern California, was asked where he thought Bishop might be.

"I think," he replied, "that he is in Yugoslavia or Croatia. He liked that area…"

Now we come to something rather puzzling and inexplicable. I call it "the mysterious letter."

On March 31, 1993, investigators for the Montgomery County Sheriff's Department announced that the previous fall they uncovered an overlooked letter addressed to Bishop that, had it been found by authorities who originally investigated the unsolved Bishop murders case, would have been a very valuable piece of evidence. The letter implied but did not directly state that Bishop might have been interested in hiring a professional killer—with the implication that it would be to kill his family. That theory, along with the possibility that Bishop had long-standing plans to dispose of the bodies in North Carolina, and planned to rendezvous with a woman in that state, stems from the letter written by an imprisoned bank robber to Bishop just before the slayings, Montgomery County Sheriff Raymond M. Kight announced. The Sheriff went on to say that if the letter had been found in a timely fashion it very well might have affected the Bishop investigation if police had been able to interview the man who wrote it, who died in 1983. The letter was found in September 1992, in Bishop's files at the State Department by Sheriff's sergeant Thomas L. Keefer and retired Montgomery County homicide detective John E. Cady, who volunteered to assist Kight after the Sheriff initiated a new look at the investigation. The failure to find the letter in the initial investigation, coupled with other evidence that was misplaced, suggests that that investigation was "somewhat slipshod," said Kight. He said county police and the FBI visited Bishop's office the day the letter was postmarked and did not learn of its existence until over fifteen years later.

The uncovered registered letter was written by bank robber A. Ken Bankston, who was at that time an inmate at the federal penitentiary in Marion, Illinois. It was postmarked March 15, 1976, and would have arrived at Bishop's office a few days later, according to Sheriff's investigators. That would have been just a day or so after Montgomery County police and the FBI had searched the office for clues. Apparently the letter was opened by a secretary and then placed in Bishop's files, which were then packed away until the investigation was re-opened. The letter makes no mention of any murder plot, but investigators believed that it might offer new insights into possible preparations for the crime that Bishop might have engaged in. The investigators were unable to find any record of other correspondence between Bishop and Bankston. But the numeral "6" was placed at the top of the letter by Bankston, and in the text were mentions of letters 4 and 5 which he said that he had written to Bishop the previous month (February 1976).

In one portion of the discovered letter Bankston wrote, "Now, in answer to your question, I am most sure that she is in a North Carolina state penitentiary." Although "she" is not identified, investigators recalled that a witness in Jacksonville, North Carolina, had reported seeing Bishop with a female companion the day after the murders, and that Bishop had used his credit card in a sporting goods store while the woman, about his age, waited outside with an Irish setter on a leash. Sergeant Keefer said that Bishop's golden retriever, Leo, had a dark coat and could have been mistaken for a setter. He and Cady set to work checking a list of all women released from North Carolina prisons during a period prior to March 1976, especially those who might have been assigned to a halfway house in or near Jacksonville.

Bankston also informed Bishop that "you could walk from Phelps Lake to Creswell. I think it is about five miles..." After checking atlases and making calls to several states, Keefer and Cady determined that Phelps Lake and Creswell are in North Carolina, just a few miles from where the bodies were found.

Keefer and Cady put in long hours, helped by the FBI, trying to track down people mentioned or referred to in the letter. After months of work they managed to locate a man mentioned in the letter only as "Sonny," who told them that he believed that Bishop had offered a passport to Bankston in return for information on how to hire a killer. The investigators say that they got conflicting answers from the State Department about whether Bishop could have been able to procure passports for himself and/or others. In his letter Bankston wrote, "I am only interested in Mexico and/or Central America, as you know." Bankston died of cancer in 1983 in Mississippi after gaining an early release from prison for medical reasons.

Another convict mentioned in the letter, David Paul Allen, told a reporter from *The Washington Post* in a telephone interview that Bishop wanted "a shooter...he was willing to spend good money and more" to kill his family. Allen was being held in jail in Salt Lake City awaiting a parole violation hearing. He further stated that Bishop "hired a couple of men to do the job, but they took off on him." Keefer believed that Allen was less than truthful and had embellished his knowledge to *The Post*. When he and Cady talked to Allen, who had been remanded to prison in Marquette, Michigan, from Salt Lake City, "He gave the impression that he did not know anything at all about Bishop." He did, however, lead investigators to several criminals who provided information similar to what Allen was taking credit for. One of them was the man referred to in the letter as "Sonny." Police would not identify Sonny, but commented that Allen identified him, also a prison inmate, as a leader of the white-supremacist Aryan Nation and the so-called Southern Mafia. Investigators cautioned that information gained from such sources must always be treated as quite likely tainted.

We now come to the "most recent" and quite possibly the last "sighting" of William Bradford Bishop, Jr., that will occur. It was in Basel, Switzerland in 1994. Sometime after the sighting a television program covering the incident was aired by NBC Television. It went as follows:

In 1994 an American couple in their early sixties was in a railway station in Basel, Switzerland. They were on a platform waiting for a train that would take them back to Zurich where their hotel was located. They were an athletic couple who had lived in Bethesda, Maryland, and had been neighbors of the Bishop family in the 1970s. While not close personal friends, they had on numerous occasions played tennis with Brad and Annette. They, like everybody in Bethesda, had followed the case closely, with a mixture of revulsion and bewilderment.

On the platform this day the husband was studying a signboard that had posted on it the schedules of various trains, including the one he was searching for and for which the couple was waiting. As he was doing this, his wife stared idly out at several rows of platforms and tracks. A train pulled into the station on the far side of the station, several platforms and tracks away, from the right, or east, direction. As the woman absently looked at the Swiss train, her attention was drawn to a man sitting by himself in a seat toward the rear, or right, of the coach directly opposite her. He was staring out the window in her direction, but not at her. He was looking at her husband very intently, as if he might have recognized him from somewhere, the woman thought. As she looked at this man who was seemingly staring at her husband, who was still inspecting the train schedules, it suddenly struck her—"My god! that's Brad Bishop!" In shock she quickly glanced away, toward her husband.

Here she interjected, "You must realize that my husband looks today remarkably as he did twenty years ago. He was tall, thin and bald then—and is so now. That was who the man I recognized as Bishop was staring at. He recognized my husband from the tennis playing days twenty years ago. I said to my husband, 'Turn slowly toward the train tracks, and look at the railway car on the farthest track directly across from us. Look casually at the man seated to the rear of the car, the one looking out the window at you, I think.'"

The husband did as suggested, turned casually and glanced at the man his wife had indicated. Then he said to her, "Good grief! That's Brad Bishop, I'm sure of it!" His wife agreed, and stated that she was as sure as she was standing there that the man in the train window across from them was Brad Bishop. She would swear to that. The woman and her husband conferred about what to do …

While they were conferring, the man evidently realized that they had become aware of them. He began to make funny faces—to disguise himself the couple thought—and then stuck his thumbs in his ears and wiggled his fingers childishly. As the couple stared at this behavior a train pulled into the station on an intervening track and the man was lost from view. Then, the couple could see his train, what appeared to be perhaps a suburban or short-haul train, pull out of the station, perhaps headed to Bern or Lausanne. As the couple's train was pulling into the station, the husband glanced quickly at the schedules posted on the signboard. One was scheduled to depart at that moment, westbound, yes, to Lausanne. Swiss trains are very prompt, he thought.

On the short ride to Zurich the couple discussed what they should do about just having seen Brad Bishop. They decided, since it was late in the afternoon and they were flying out of Zurich early the next morning, to wait until they got back to Washington D.C., and then they would report the sighting the very next morning to the FBI. Which is what they did.

Early on the morning after they got back they made an appointment with an FBI agent, who said that he would see them right away. In the agent's office they told their story very carefully and with great accuracy, even down to the time and what train the husband thought Bishop might have been on headed west or south. The agent took very methodical notes, asked quite a few other questions, thanked them profoundly for what he said was "very significant and important information." And showed them out of the office.

The couple watched the news very carefully for the next few weeks, even European papers that were available in Washington. There was nothing about Bishop, no news of the sighting, and certainly nothing about him being apprehended. They wondered if somehow it was all being handled very quietly, secretly even. After weeks of silence they surmised that somehow Bishop had slipped away from Switzerland, perhaps after suspecting that he might have been recognized there in Basel by his former tennis playing friends.

The last piece of material connected to Bishop surfaced in April 2004, when a woman in North Carolina reported buying a diary that had been written by Bishop. She said that she purchased the item at a yard sale. Investigators said that the last entry was well before the murders, and that there was nothing in the content of the diary that was helpful.

X.

MR. "X"

What actually inspired me to make a second telephone call to Detective Cady was the airing of a television show about the last sighting of Bishop, in Basel, Switzerland. Although the sighting had been in 1994, the television show did not appear until late 1998. Hoffman made a taped copy of the show and invited me out to view it. We watched that show several times and commented at length about it. Hoffman was convinced that the sighting was legitimate, that the older couple had seen Bishop, and that he was still a fugitive somewhere, if not in Switzerland. I, being a natural skeptic, was not so sure. I asked Hoffman to make a copy of the show for me, and I sent that tape to a friend in New York City who is a neurosurgeon and a psychiatrist asking him to review it and give me his analysis. A few weeks later he reported back to me that in his professional opinion the older couple had not seen Bishop—they THOUGHT they had, were CONVINCED that they had, but were simply mistaken. His reasoning? He said, "A fugitive does not behave the way they described the man in the train window behaving. He does not call attention to himself in that manner. The man in the train window saw the couple evidently staring at him and made faces, that's all." But what about the man initially staring at the husband on the platform? "Just a Swiss man wondering if he knew that chap. Nothing more…" So, I rather concluded that the Basel sighting was a case of mistaken identity. There had been no Brad Bishop on a train in Switzerland.

Sometime in early 1999 I decided to make the call to Detective Cady. He had nothing new to offer, and indeed was a bit curt with me on the telephone, as if I was pestering him. I think, however, that it was his frustration with the case. I asked him about the Basel sighting and the TV program. He said that it was interesting but it had not produced anything. I asked if he thought Bishop could be in South America, and he said that he had always liked that. I started to ask something else, but he interrupted me and said, "Listen. Why don't you call this guy—he knows more about this case than anyone…" He gave me a name and a telephone number, and hung up. A guy "who knows more about this case than anyone?" That certainly sounded intriguing. I made the call.

After several rings a woman's voice answered pleasantly, informing me that I had reached—and repeated the number that I had called. She asked with whom did I wish to speak and what about? When I had offered the information she said that he would call me back—evidently there was caller ID. A few minutes later my telephone rang and when I answered a rather cultivated man's voice asked if he was speaking to Dayton Lummis? Ah, the marvels of technology. I informed him that he was, and he asked what my interest was in William Bradford Bishop, Jr. I told him that Detective Cady had suggested that I call— and he said quietly, "Cady, good man."—and I explained that Bishop had been my roommate senior year in college, but I had had no contact with him since 1964. However, I had been following the case in the newspapers with avid interest, and had many questions, doubts even, about the whole matter. He sort of chuckled and said, "As do many…" I am going to call this man "Mr. X" in order to protect his identity.

Although I had been given a name to ask for, I would say that was undoubtedly not a true name. Nonetheless, because of his sensitive position it is best not to suggest any identity of any sort.

We chatted a bit more and then he asked me if I believed that Bishop had killed his whole family and had been a fugitive ever since. To be safe I answered that that certainly was what the circumstantial evidence strongly suggested. He then asked me where I thought Bishop might be at that time, or most recently. When I said, "At the bottom of a West Virginia coal mine," there was a long pause. It was then that I mentioned that I had a sort of gut feeling that Bishop had not been alive for a very long time, not since somewhat after the killings. "Interesting," he said. "And what do you think might have happened?" I went on to tell him that I thought that some time not long after the killings "someone" got hold of Bishop "and deep sixed him". "Deep sixed," he repeated. And I said, "You know, like terminated with extreme prejudice." He asked if I had a military background. I told him just enough to be familiar with the terminology. He went on to ask why I thought that might have happened and who did it? I tread carefully in explaining that something might have come up in Bishop's career that made him a liability to the State Department "or possibly others." I mentioned the theory that Bishop could not be brought to trial or tried in absentia, because of things that might be brought out. Thus, I mentioned to him, a title for anything that I might write on the Bishop case, "NOT WANTED." He laughed and said that was clever, Then he asked my why did I think "these people" might have terminated Bishop? Well, I told him that in addition to not wanting a trial they figured the man had committed a horrible crime, so why not serve as judge, jury and executioner? He said that was all very interesting but that he did not, could not, agree with it. Why not? Because of the most recent sighting, the one in Basel.

He proceeded to tell me that he considered the first two sightings, the one in Sweden and the one in Italy, to be spurious, and why. The woman in Sweden, he said, while she had known Bishop in Ethiopia, was not accurate in her identity of various photos of Bishop. Plus, the Swedish authorities considered her to be somewhat unstable. Hence, they concluded "No Bishop," and Mr. X concurred. The sighting in Italy, the one by a man who had been a co-worker of Bishop, also had problems. The man who reported the sighting was also unstable, and investigators concluded that he had made up the sighting to call attention to himself. Thus, said Mr. X, those sightings can be discounted. But, the sighting in Basel, that is a different matter, he said, and went on to discuss that sighting in some detail. I told him that a friend had made a copy of the TV program and I had watched it several times. I did not tell him of my doctor friend's analysis of the tape and his conclusion.

He said that the older American couple who had played tennis with Bishop in Bethesda were extremely reliable, had excellent eyesight, and had stated that they had gotten very good, unimpeded looks at the man they identified. No doubt about it in their minds, they had seen William Bradford Bishop, Jr. And Mr. X believed them implicitly. They had absolutely no reason to make anything up. I mentioned that I wondered about the man putting his thumbs in his ears and wiggling his fingers if he thought that they recognized him. That sounded a little fanciful. Mr. X said that he did not know about that, but according to the couple the last they saw of the man they identified as Bishop was him standing up, locking his eyes on theirs, and waving. Then his train pulled out. Why, I asked Mr. X, would he do that? Don't know, he said, perhaps he was mocking them and the world and knew that he could disappear immediately. Where? Perhaps Eastern Europe. I remembered that Annette Bishop's brother had suggested to investigators that they might look for Bishop in Croatia, that "he had liked that area." Well, yeah, he might have liked it but did somebody there not like him? Who knew? Mr. X thought Croatia might be an excellent place to hide.

The couple told all this to the FBI in Washington immediately upon their return the next day. But, said Mr. X, "Here is where things get a little strange, and may play just a bit into your conspiracy theory. After the couple made their report to a very polite and meticulous agent, nothing was done. The police chief in Basel was not notified, the Swiss National Police were not notified, INTERPOL was not notified—all very much at odds with procedure when such a fugitive is sighted. A world-wide alert would go out, both to national police agencies and to INTERPOL to be on lookout for such and such fugitive. For someone of Bishop's 'stature' the level of alert would be at the very highest." But, said Mr. X, in this case nothing was done. Or so it seemed. Very strange. Inexplicable. Or was it?

"Now," said Mr. X, "at the risk of buying into, at least partially, your conspiracy theory, that Bishop was somehow 'terminated by persons or entities unknown', the possibility exists that when the couple made their report to the FBI, there was some sort of 'little red flag' indicating something like 'Take no action—this has been dealt with...' A possibility that cannot be excluded. But this would mean that the couple was mistaken, and I do not think they were. So that leaves—what?"

"One other possibility is that without notifying any other agencies, the FBI/CIA/whoever else initiated a surreptitious investigation and search. And in so doing possibly did locate and secretively apprehend Bishop. And then remanded him to some foreign and remote location for 'debriefing and termination.' All very secretive. Possible. But it is very hard to keep a complete lid on things like that. Just as it would be with your initial theory. Someone almost always talks. If they can, that is."

"Or, there is always the possibility that they never found him. That he quickly disappeared to, say, Croatia—which is not all that far from Switzerland. So, where are we left? With a lot of questions and no answers. Now, I want to confuse you a little more and ask what you know about Bishop's military career, what he did before the State Department?"

I said that I knew that Bishop had enlisted in the army right after graduating from Yale, that he had studied at the Army Language School in Monterey, California, and that he had further studied the Serbo-Croatian language at what I thought was the University of Padua in Italy but seems to have been the University of Verona. And then spent his Army career in Army Intelligence listening to radio broadcasts out of Yugoslavia, being discharged in 1963 with only a good conduct medal. But, I added, I had run into a fellow Yale classmate, also in Army Intelligence, who had once visited with Bishop in Italy, and Bishop had let drop that he "was running a guy in Yugoslavia". Nothing further was said on this matter, but my classmate had the notion that Bishop was handling an informant. Mr. X listened to this and commented, "Superficially, and unofficially, quite correct. But the situation was rather more complicated. What do you know about what was going on in Yugoslavia circa 1960, Croatia specifically?" Just a bit, I told him. That amounts of gold, jewels, art objects, much of it loot from World War Two, were being smuggled out of Yugoslavia to Bari, Italy, and on to Naples, where organized crime had a hand in all this. Perhaps something to do with Croatian nationalism. A bit murky, I am afraid. Mr. X agreed, and said that it was a nasty piece of business, the Croats and their fanatical nationalism. Then, too, there was the fear by the West that Russia might invade Yugoslavia to get the country firmly back into the Soviet sphere. Mr. X commented that U.S. Army Intelligence had quite an interest in all of this, and that Bishop had played a role, perhaps a significant one. He thought that Bishop had been chosen early on at Fort Holabird for some kind of Balkan role, because of his appearance, which was admittedly rather Serb, or Slavic.

Mr. X told me that Bishop had made at least two incursions into Yugoslavia, and that for one of those he had been awarded a citation for bravery. Mr. X asked me if I understood the term "incursion?" I said that I did—"A hostile entrance into a territory, like a raid..." Very good, commented Mr. X, and he went on to explain that the U.S. Army did not award citations for bravery lightly. That bravery meant coming under fire, facing extreme danger, accomplishing a very hazardous mission, etc. Something very serious. So, Bishop did something inside Yugoslavia, something significant. "Then Bishop was discharged from the army in late 1963, studied at Middlebury College in Vermont and got a Master's degree, returned to California where you saw him, when, in late 1964?" I affirmed that this was correct.

Mr. X went on: "Then, evidently, somewhere along the line he had applied to the State Department, which can be a cover for all sorts of things. While he was being vetted and so forth, evidently in the summer of 1965 he and Annette took a rather extended 'tourist trip' throughout Yugoslavia, which was a very historical and attractive if primitive country. Speaking the language fluently, knowing the customs, they would have no problem fitting in and functioning. When Bishop returned from Yugoslavia in the late summer of 1965 he went to visit a man in Germany who was a sort of 'sponsor,' an experienced diplomat who had interviewed Bishop and recommended him. Evidently this man knew about the tourist trip to Yugoslavia and was furious. He told Bishop, 'By visiting that country you have done a very, very seriously stupid thing. You exposed yourself to the possibility of very serious personal harm, and/or harm to your wife. And you also risked the possibility of an extremely serious international incident.' The man threatened to derail any State Department career then and there, but evidently somehow the incident got smoothed over and Bishop went on the be accepted at State Department that fall."

I found all this quite interesting, and was not surprised when Mr. X told me that today all of this army record or other stuff would be "unavailable," wiped off the record. The sponsor was now dead. But, he—Mr. X—had been years earlier able to get hold of a lot of stuff that was no longer available and file it away. Bishop was one of his projects, though he did not exactly put it that way. He asked me what my interpretation of these events was. I told him that there could be only one interpretation. That Bishop did something very serious inside Yugoslavia. Killed or kidnapped somebody. And then, when he took that tourist trip he risked being recognized by someone, a former adversary, victim's family member, or someone "on the other side," who would either kill him out of vengeance, attempt to do so, or kill his wife—a form of Balkan justice. Or, he could have been arrested in Yugoslavia for some sort of "war crime" and subjected to "a circus trial" which would have been very embarrassing to the United States. Neither likelihood was something either the State Department or Bishop would want. Hence the accusation of extremely poor judgment. Mr. X agreed with all this, and wondered if whatever Bishop did in Yugoslavia could have arisen at the time he was up for the promotion that he failed to get? He said that things have a way of being dragged around behind one and surfacing at inconvenient times. That could have very well been the case with Bishop. I had to wonder why Mr. X brought up this military background. Superficially, events in Yugoslavia might seem to have nothing to do with the Bishop killings. Or did they?

As we neared the end of our telephone conversation, which lasted over an hour, Mr. X dropped a few more tidbits about the Bishop case. For instance, he said that right away the "CIA Damage Control Squad" had been called in. Then this was covered up. He also told me that at the Federal level incorrect Social Security and passport numbers had been recorded for Bishop, which I found very puzzling. What the implication of this was, he did not elaborate on. He also told me that the psychiatrist that Bishop had been seeing was a Coast Guard psychiatrist, which would seem to be some sort of cover. The final matter that he touched on was mysterious letter from Bangston discovered in 1992, and the five previous ones alluded to. He rather dismissed those letters, saying that they might have had to do with something Bishop was working on outside the parameter of his regular job description. That might have been significant. But, again, he did not elaborate.

We had one more, shorter conversation after January 1999, but there was nothing new. Then, a few months passed and I had a few other matters that I thought I would like to discuss. When I called the number I had and asked for him I was told that he "was unavailable." When I asked when he would be available I was told that was information not available at this time. I left my name and number, and asked that he call me about the William Bradford Bishop, Jr., case. No call ever came…

A few weeks later I tried again to contact Mr. X, with the same result. He never called me. I knew that he never would. Had he grown tired of talking to me? Or had he been "Shut down"? Perhaps said too much, or was leading attention in uncomfortable directions. Impossible to tell. I had no reason to disbelieve anything that the man told me. He was obviously in some sort of high and sensitive position to know things. I thought of calling Detective Cady to ask about Mr. X, but decided that would be another stone wall. I thought about the things Mr. X told me. Although he had not said so directly, I had the definite opinion that he considered Bishop guilty of murdering his family, and that he had escaped to become a fugitive. But he had never mentioned anything like a motive. I also had the very strong feeling that he had unresolved questions about the whole case, things that could not be rationally put together and explained. He did seem to believe in the Basel sighting, but wondered if anything had been done about it. I rather thought he leaned toward the notion that something had, secretly and quietly. He gave the impression of a man who understood how those things worked.

So, where was I left? With not much. Except the Yugoslavia connection—if there was one. I decided to learn more about that country, about Croatia specifically, since that was where most of the intrigue was emanating from, and it was a place that Bishop had said that "he liked." I thought of Maria Begovic and her paranoia, of Dr. Avis at the flag shop who had mentioned Croatian customers that he thought had Ustache connections. I thought of gold, jewels and art works being smuggled out of Yugoslavia, possibly to support some future Croatian nationalism. And I thought of the sordid World War Two period when Croatia was firmly in the Nazi camp under the fascist iron fist of Ante Pavelic, Hitler's stooge. I decided to focus on him in my investigations into Croatia. As it turned out, a rather interesting and good choice.

XI.

COUNSEL FOR THE DEFENSE

In this chapter I am going to ask a number of very direct questions, to which there will be a simple yes or no answer. Then I shall return to these questions for some brief discussion and clarification. Following that will be a series of what I call secondary questions pertinent to what has been developed or put forth by the primary questions. I shall suggest the possibility of alternatives to the line of reasoning and accusation developed by the investigators. Whether one agrees or not is not the question. What is being asked is "Can certain allegations be proven beyond reasonable doubt?", and, "Are certain alternative things possible?"

Questions:

1. Can it be proven beyond reasonable doubt that William Bradford Bishop, Jr.,—hereafter referred to as "Defendant"—was physically present at the Bishop house in Bethesda at the time when the killings of the five members of the Bishop family took place? No!

2. Can it be proven beyond reasonable doubt that defendant removed or caused to be removed the five bodies and placed them in the family Chevy Malibu station wagon? No!

3. Can it be proven beyond reasonable doubt that defendant drove the station wagon containing the five bodies through the night almost 300 miles to a remote location 6 miles south of Columbia, North Carolina? No!

4. Can it be proven beyond reasonable doubt that defendant in that remote spot dug a shallow grave, removed said bodies from the station wagon, placed them in the shallow grave, poured gasoline on them and set them afire? No!

5. Can it be proven beyond reasonable doubt that defendant appeared in late afternoon of the day the bodies were discovered at a sporting goods store in Jacksonville, North Carolina, and used his credit card for a purchase in the amount of $15.60? Yes!

6. Can it be proven beyond reasonable doubt that a woman seen by the proprietor of said store who was holding a dog on a leash outside said store was in any way waiting for, connected to, or in any way involved with defendant? No!

7. Can it be proven beyond reasonable doubt that defendant drove the Chevy Malibu station wagon to the west side of Great Smoky Mountains National Park and there abandoned it? No!

8. Can it be proven beyond reasonable doubt that defendant was at any time before and after the discovery of the station wagon physically in or anywhere near the discovery location, or anywhere else in the National Park? No!

9. Can it be proven beyond reasonable doubt that defendant did not leave by vessel, either willingly or unwillingly, from either of the ports of Jacksonville or Wilmington, North Carolina, and proceeded to or was taken to someplace unknown for reasons not known at this time? No!

10. Can it be proven beyond reasonable doubt that following defendant's disappearance in March of 1976 that he was alive and a fugitive at least through 1994? No!

What we have here so far is what some might consider a rather compelling body of testimony that would lay groundwork for the acquittal of defendant in spite of the seeming overwhelming circumstantial evidence against him. One is not supposed to be convicted solely by circumstantial evidence but it does happen, however. When seeking defendant's indictment before a grand jury, in addition to the overwhelming circumstantial evidence just two pieces of factual evidence were presented. And here we must remember the old adage that you can get a grand jury to indict a ham sandwich. The two pieces of factual evidence were a single finger print lifted from the gasoline can found at the gravesite, and bloody finger and palm prints at the murder scene that were identified as defendant's. We shall get back to these, but first a few secondary questions must be asked, and in so doing it will be seen that grounds for an alternative theory what might have occurred are emerging.

1. Can it be proven beyond reasonable doubt that person or persons unknown did not present to the State Department evidence of some very damaging nature concerning something that defendant did in his career, either with the Army or with the State Department, revelation of such damaging nature that his promotion was denied, his career placed in jeopardy, and possible criminal action made a very real possibility? No!

2. Can it be proven beyond reasonable doubt that person or persons unknown with this information did not have power and a hold over defendant, and order or otherwise coerce defendant to make the purchases of gas can and hammer at Sears, and subsequent filling of car and can, and withdrawal of money from bank? No!

3. Can it be proven beyond reasonable doubt that such person or persons unknown did not order or otherwise coerce defendant to leave his house in a suit around 10:30 p.m., telling his wife that he had important State Department business and that someone would be picking him up outside? No!

4. Can it be proven beyond reasonable doubt that upon leaving his house at approximately 10:30 p.m. and being picked up by person

or persons unknown, defendant was not restrained and injected with a sedative, rendering him comatose and unconscious for a protracted period of time? No!

At this point there will be those who will be saying that this is all pretty far-fetched, and perhaps with good reason. The points being made here are just the "no" answers, the lack of proof beyond reasonable doubt, which is, after all, what a trial is all about.

As for defendant allegedly not being in the house at the time the murders were committed, there is no witness or witnesses to place him there. And there is no murder weapon to connect defendant with the crimes. It is often said that in a homicide trial, no murder weapon no case. That is not true, however. Circumstantial evidence may be so powerful that a conviction can be voted for. That was evidently the strategy of the authorities in this case.

Of the two pieces of factual evidence presented to the grand jury, one was the SINGLE fingerprint lifted from the gas can. Defendant bought the can—of course his prints would be on it. Why just one identifiable? Was the person handling the can at the gravesite wearing gloves, which obliterated other prints? Likewise with the shovel and pitchfork. No mention of any fingerprints from those implements. If they were garden tools at the Bishop home one would think that defendant's prints would be all over them. Were they and the can handled by person or persons unknown who did not want THEIR prints found and/or identified. and those items were wiped down? Quite possibly...

As for the bloody finger and palm prints on the wall of the Bishop house, these would appear to be quite condemnatory. Those prints were closely examined and analyzed by a number of experts, who had rather differing conclusions about them. Some questioned the manner with which the prints were placed on the wall. The essential question was—could it be proven beyond reasonable doubt that a conscious and functioning defendant did cause his bloodied fingers and palms to transfer clear and identifiable prints to the wall of the house? No! Experts testified that it was clearly within the realm of possibility that an unconscious, non-functional defendant having been injected with a powerful sedative, was brought into the house briefly, had his fingers and palms smeared with victims' blood and placed against the wall. One might find that far-fetched, but again it cannot be proven beyond reasonable doubt not to have happened.

As for removal of the bodies from the house, and the transporting of them to rural North Carolina, again no witnesses, no singular or definitive pieces of evidence. Only the circumstance and "Of course he killed them and drove the bodies to North Carolina. Who else could have done it? Defendant had motive, means, and opportunity!" Well, sort of. Of these three classic components of homicide prosecution, in this case no clear, persuasive or compelling motive was ever established. Only vague psychological theories about people mentally "disassembling," cracking up, going off the deep end doing something "horrible" and then not remembering anything about it. All extremely vague, none of it particularly pertinent to this case. It leaves us with the thinking that if defendant did indeed commit the crimes of which he is suspected, why on earth did he do it? There is considerably more logic to the thinking that "He could not have done it." But, speculation is neither helpful nor permissible here...

The question remains—"If defendant did not commit the crimes of which he was accused, who did, and why?" We shall be getting back to that question. But first, a few more questions.

1. Why did defendant show up at the sporting goods store in Jacksonville? There is simply no good explanation for this, other than perhaps the one about the town being a port. That town is certainly not on the way to Great Smoky National Park from Columbia, North Carolina. And what did he buy for $15.60? Some small items for a change in plan, whatever that might have been? And why neat-appearing, politely-spoken, and wearing a suit? Not the demeanor of a

man who has just killed his entire family, attempted to burn and bury their bodies. Not at all. Could defendant in some way not have known what had happened, being just awakened from a sedative that perhaps had been injected into him? Was the "dark skinned woman" perhaps "a minder" of some sort, and was defendant still under the influence of some sort of drug, hence his calm and pleasant demeanor?

2. Why would a fugitive use a credit card so casually? It defies logic that he would, unless he was unaware of being a fugitive. Or something…

It was naturally assumed that defendant himself abandoned the station wagon on the west side of the National Park, although there is no logical explanation for this choice of location. As mentioned by Detective Cady the bloodhounds followed "a trail" about a half mile into the forest, back again to the parking lot, where the trail circled around a bit and abruptly stopped in the middle of the lot. Cady and the other investigators concluded that defendant at that spot got into a vehicle driven by some sort of collaborator or rescuer, hard as it might be to think of someone who would play that role.

But, if it cannot be proven beyond reasonable doubt the defendant was ever in that vicinity, what about the trail? Well, clothes with defendant's scent could have been dragged about, for reasons unknown but evidently to establish the notion of his presence in that locale. Or perhaps to add to the growing mystique of the defendant's complete disappearance. Or to deflect attention away from either Jacksonville or Wilmington and any thought that defendant left from either of those ports, either willingly or unwillingly, in the latter case with the speculation that he was in some way under the control of person or persons unknown.

Further, we must question the items found in the abandoned vehicle, the shotgun and shells, the men's clothing, etc. Could it be that these items were chosen by defendant for a plan that underwent a sudden change? Or were the items simply to create the illusion of a fugitive? Whatever the case, it was decided, either by defendant or person or persons unknown, that these items were no longer needed. A change of plan.

Now we must return to the very beginning of this sad and tragic episode, and engage in some speculation surrounding the purchase of the gasoline can and the hammer, etc. Is it possible that defendant was told that these items were for some purpose that did not concern him and not to worry about it? Instructed to just leave the items in the car. Possibly…

And now, can it be proven beyond reasonable doubt that person or persons unknown who had power and influence over defendant did not inform him that information about crimes and violations defendant had committed in his career had been given to the State Department and that was why he did get promoted? That his career was over and he would be facing criminal charges, would be made an example of, be convicted and sent to federal prison. That his family would be forever shamed and humiliated. That his sons would always carry the stain of their father's crimes and political instability. BUT, defendant could have been informed that there was a way out of this, a way to save his family from shame and humiliation, perhaps even to save his own reputation. And that would be for defendant to "quietly disappear." That defendant could be spirited to a remote foreign country, with an altered identity, and there begin a new life and live quietly. The State Department would probably be happy to have defendant just "disappear," and save the bother of a lengthy and troublesome trial. Defendant might be told that his family were resilient people, that they could adjust and go on. Perhaps believing that somehow old enemies of defendant caught up with him and defendant died somehow in the service of his country, Any number of things could be believed.

Can it be proven beyond reasonable doubt that nothing like the above took place? No! Farfetched as it might seem, therein lies a plausible theory, up to a point. There follows a twist in this whole matter, and that is the murders of the Bishop family members. Did person or persons unknown dupe defendant into thinking that in some strange way they were helping him out of a seemingly dead-end situation, when in reality they had something entirely different and brutal in mind for him? Let us explore what that might have been, and how it might have taken place...

XII.

THE CROATIAN "FACTOR"

We remember that Annette Bishop's brother suggested to the authorities that they look for Bishop in Croatia, that "he seemed to like it there." Meaning, of course, that Bishop had talked favorably about Croatia, quite likely from the time he and his wife spent in Yugoslavia as tourists in 1965. But, he most certainly did not discuss his two incursions into Yugoslavia, one of which he was awarded a citation for bravery. These incursions would have been initiated along the coast, which was Croatian. A citation for bravery is not given lightly by the United States Army. It entails having come under fire, accomplishing something very dangerous, risking life and limb on a mission. So, it is very likely that Bishop did something quite serious in Yugoslavia, in Croatia. Perhaps killed someone. The fact that his sponsor for "the State Department" in Germany was so upset when he learned about the tourist visit with his wife to Yugoslavia is quite significant. That he told Bishop that he had been incredibly stupid visiting that country, that he had exposed himself to "the risk of serious personal harm, and/or the possibility of a very serious international incident." We assume that the "serious personal harm" remark meant that someone in Yugoslavia/Croatia might have recognized Bishop and decided to take revenge by killing him and/or his wife. The international incident would probably involve Bishop being arrested for some crime committed in Yugoslavia/Croatia, and being subjected to a "show trial." The revenge factor might seem most significant in retrospect.

The fact that treasure—gold, gems, jewelry, cash and art works stolen during the Nazi (Ustache) period during World War II from Jews, Gypsies, Serbs and Muslims in Croatia—was being smuggled out after the war to Bari, Italy, on to Naples and into the hands of organized crime was of interest to U.S. Army Intelligence. In the early 1960s investigation and interdiction of that very well might have involved Bishop. The smuggling and fund raising were being carried out by Ustache operatives seeking to raise funds for the on-going struggle of the cause of Croatian nationalism. Interference with those operations would have been quite dangerous.

U.S. Army Intelligence was also interested in the remnants of the Ustache, underground groups in Croatia made up of former Nazi party members and sympathizers. These were seen as an element of resistance to Communism, both within Yugoslavia and from without—i.e. the Soviet Union. It was feared that the Soviets might invade Yugoslavia to bring it more firmly into the Soviet orbit. This was one of the big Cold War fears. Thus Ustache operatives and others had to be monitored inside Yugoslavia. We remember that Bishop had told his college friend that he "was running a guy in Yugoslavia." Doubtless, the extent of his activities within that country was much more extensive than would have been thought. So much so, one might presume, as to make him seen as a distinct "enemy of the state," and an appropriate target for Ustache/Balkan revenge.

It must be understood that of the so-called Balkan countries, Croatia, along with Slovenia, is a Roman Catholic country, as opposed to the Orthodox Serbs and others to the south, and is culturally oriented north to Austria and northern European countries. This has long engendered a sense to superiority over the Serbs (Maria Begovic—"Serbs—All Gypsies!"), exacerbated by the historic position of power held by the Serbs. In recent times Croatians have suffered extreme domination and brutal injustices at the hands of the Serbs. For a brief period during World War II when the Nazi Ustache party was in power the tables were turned and it was the Serbs who were brutalized. A long history of bitterness in that part of the world.

The fires of Croatian nationalism burned, and continue to burn, with considerable force, with great longing for the last Croatian kingdom under the supposed beneficent, peaceful and prosperous reign of Zvonomir the First, last King of Croatia, who ruled from 1075 to 1089. Balkan memories are long! Much of this ardent nationalism has devolved into a sort of fanaticism, with dangerous ramifications. And often with a maniacal desire for revenge against those believed to have acted against their cause and their personages. A dangerous force indeed. This must be recognized if one is to understand what these people are capable of. We see in Bishop's career with U.S. Army Intelligence (and possibly later, if Bishop was indeed a spy/clandestine operative involved with ongoing Yugoslav investigations) a number of points of intersection with possible violent Croatian nationalists where acts committed by him might very well have targeted him for some unique form of "Balkan revenge." If by this time the reader is wondering if I will be suggesting some possible—and I stress possible—sort of "Balkan connection" to the Bishop case, that would be a reasonable speculation.

But first it is necessary to understand a very brief resume of Croatian history since World War I.

In the last half of the nineteenth century, and up to World War I, Croatia was part of the Austro-Hungarian Empire and enjoyed considerable and rather unusual autonomy. When the Empire collapsed in 1918 and was broken up, Croatia was absorbed into something called "The Kingdom of the Serbs, Croats and Slovenes." This kingdom was ruled by a Serbian monarch in Belgrade, and was dominated completely by Serb Orthodox Catholics. Under this Kingdom, which was never approved or ratified by the Croatian parliament, the Croats were deprived of their national rights and had unreasonably high taxes imposed on them. All decisions and decrees emanated from Belgrade and a government made up of 90 percent Serbs.

By 1927/28 discontent in Croatia had reached a critical point, and the people united in opposition to Serbian domination. The most powerful group was the Croatian Peasant Party. In retaliation for a number of violent incidents, Belgrade took the opportunity to assassinate Croatian parliamentary leader Stjepan Radic, and a few others. There followed a period of mass persecution and massacres of Croats by the Serbs. Many Croatian nationalists fled abroad, many to the United States, to continue to agitate for the Croatian cause. One was a rising charismatic leader, Ante Pavelic, who in Italy in 1932 founded a strident nationalist movement called "The Ustache," the avowed purpose of which was the destruction of the Yugoslav state and the establishment of a free and independent Croatia. This group attempted an "invasion" of the Kingdom of Yugoslavia in 1932, but this failed almost before it began. Ante Pavelic remained in Italy, briefly "under arrest," but in reality under the benevolent protection of Mussolini—who always knew a dedicated fascist when he saw one.

In 1929 the Serbs established a single Kingdom of Yugoslavia, under the monarch King Alexander. Ante Pavelic and the Ustache teamed up with Macedonian dissidents and assassinated this king in Marseilles, France, in 1935. The kingdom was then administered by a team of three Serb regents in Belgrade, who steered the country away from France and Europe, and steadily toward Fascism, i.e. Mussolini and Adolf Hitler.

The Croatian Peasant Party grew increasingly powerful, and eventually pressured the regency in Belgrade to permit the establishment of the Banate, or State, of Croatia, allowing the citizens considerable autonomy and some of the benefits of statehood.

All that was to be rendered moot, however, by the outbreak of World War II.

In early 1941 Yugoslavia entered into a tripartite pact with Italy and Germany. This quickly unraveled, however, due to British intervention and pressures. Thus, Germany was provided with an excuse to invade Yugoslavia, which it did and quickly crushed all resistance in twelve days. The Germans set about partitioning the country, and in so doing formed the Independent State of Croatia. Italy was permitted to acquire many miles of the Croatian coastline.

With the blessings of Mussolini, Ante Pavelic and a band of Ustache returned to Croatia after many years of exile. The German occupiers assisted Pavelic in seizing power and consolidating it under the Ustache. Thus did Ante Pavelic become "the Poglavnic of Croatia," in effect Hitler's surrogate in that country. The Ustache proved to be a brutal fascist regime, and initiated a program of ethnic cleansing so cruel that several German Nazis were appalled. Hundreds of thousands of Jews, Serbs, Roma, Muslims, and any others deemed to be unsuitable to a pure Roman Catholic Croatian state were rounded up, placed in concentration camps and mostly executed. Vast amounts of cash, gold, jewels, gems and valuable pieces of art were appropriated and hidden by the Ustache. Estimates of executed victims were: 30,000 Jews, 30,000 Gypsies, and somewhere between 300,000 and 600,000 Serbs. The Serbs were particularly hated because of their previous treatment of Croatia. These horrendous crimes were so excessive as to earn Ante Pavelic the name "Butcher of the Balkans." Assisting in this brutal scheme was a Catholic priest, Father Krunoslav Dragonavic, who was a high official in the Ministry for Internal Colonization. This entity was responsible for murdering tens of thousands, seizing their assets, and expelling hundreds of thousands from Croatia. All this took place under the protection of the German occupiers. In 1943 Father Dragonavic was sent to the Vatican as a representative of the Croatian Red Cross.

By 1944 Marshal Tito and his communist partisans, with Russian and British assistance, began to gain power in the south of Yugoslavia. They took Belgrade and began a final assault on Croatia. When the war in Europe ended in May of 1945 with the surrender of Germany, the German forces had already withdrawn from Croatia. The Croatian army fell apart and surrendered. Many soldiers fled to Austria where the British gathered them up and handed them over to the Yugoslav partisans. They were then put in concentration camps, many of the same ones where they had held Serbs, and eventually executed in great numbers, in revenge for the Croatian slaughter of Serbs under the Ustache regime. Large numbers of Croat civilians fled over the mountains to Austria (Maria Begovic) and a great many eventually found their way to the United States, where they continued to agitate for Croatian independence. Many high ranking Ustache, such as Ante Pavelic, were assisted by the Vatican and Father Dragonavic in escaping, most of them eventually to South America. The treasure stolen from Ustache victims was not located, and to this day is hunted for. Marshal Tito crushed Croatia when incorporating it into the Yugoslav Socialist Federation, and the Croats were once again reduced to inferior status by the dominant Orthodox Serbs ruling from Belgrade.

Tito had promised to respect states rights in Croatia when his communist regime seized power, but in reality that never came to pass. All army, police and diplomatic positions in the Yugoslav Federation were held by Serbs. Many Croatians were forced to resign from these factions, and were imprisoned or liquidated. The Roman Catholic Church was persecuted, and Arch-Bishop Stepinac was sentenced to life imprisonment for "crimes against the State." By 1971 Croatian discontent reached such a critical level that strident demands were made to Belgrade for more independence and rights. This was brutally crushed by Tito. Thousands of Croats were imprisoned, killed or forced to emigrate—many to the Untied States where they set up groups to raise money (often through criminal acts) to further the cause of Croatian independence, Many of these groups were headed by former Ustache members, or strong sympathizers to the movement. All this contributed to a somewhat fanatical rising tide of Croatian nationalist sentiment.

Ante Pavelic escaped into Austria, and with the assistance of Father Draganovic bribed his way into being sheltered by the Vatican. He was rumored to be in control of much of the Ustache treasure stolen from its victims. For a period of time Pavelic lived more or less openly, disguised as a priest. In 1948 the Vatican and Father Draganovic assisted Ante Pavelic in reaching Argentina, where he obtained a position as security advisor to President Juan Peron. By 1948 "the ratline" established by Father Draganovic had succeeded in assisting 7250 former Ustache members in escaping to South America. Much of this was done with United States awareness and/or approval.

While Ante Pavelic was living in Buenos Aires, the Yugoslav "secret police" identified him, caught up with him and severely wounded him in an assassination attempt. He seemed to recover sufficiently to assume a position in 1959 as "Minister of Interior Security" in the regime of "El Benefactor," President Alfredo Stroessner of Paraguay. His recovery proved to be less than complete, however, and he went to Madrid for further medical treatment. He died in that city in 1959, and his body remains there in a secret location, guarded by loyal members of the Ustache, awaiting the time when it can be taken back to Zagreb and buried with honors. So far permission to do this has been refused by past and present administrators in Croatia (as reported by United States Army Intelligence.) It is rumored that much of his treasure is in Madrid, controlled by relatives of the Poglavnic. Several class action lawsuits have been initiated to attempt to return at least parts of this vast treasure to the heirs of rightful owners.

Father Draganivic continued to operate under the protection of the Vatican, helping former Nazis escape to South America. In 1958, however, due to international pressure the Vatican asked him to leave and cut all ties with him. He set up an intelligence operation in Rome, and hired out his services to a number of countries. The United States willingly employed him, with full knowledge of his brutal Nazi/Ustache background, and even sponsored a trip to Cleveland, Ohio, to give a speech extolling Croatian nationalism. In 1962, United States Army Intelligence finally fired him as being "too unreliable." He then slipped back into Yugoslavia, where he praised Tito, denounced the Ustache and his former association. Amazingly, he was not arrested but was allowed to live quietly in a monastery outside Sarajevo where he died quietly in 1983.

During the 1960s and 70s there were numerous Croatian nationalist groups operating in the United States, most prominently in Cleveland and the San Francisco Bay Area (Maria Begovic again). They were in nature ultra-nationalist, and marked by ethnic/religious fanaticism. According to FBI reports many of these groups were engaged in criminal activity for fund raising—bombings, extortion, bank robberies among them.

In 1975 a bomb went off at LaGuardia Airport in New York, killing eleven persons and wounding many more. Although that crime has never been solved, many investigators think there might have been a Croatian involvement. The next year a TWA plane was hijacked by one Zvonko Busic and three Croatian accomplices. To give credence to his act, Busic had placed a bomb in a locker at Grand Central Station in New York. This exploded while New York Police bomb squad officers were attempting to disarm it. One officer was killed and another blinded. Busic was sentenced to life in prison, but was released in 2008 after 32 years. He returned to Croatia, where he was given a hero's welcome.

Also in 1976 the Yugoslav embassy in Washington, D.C. was bombed by Croatian Nationalists/terrorists.

In 1981 Ustache sympathizers set off a bomb in the Statue of Liberty in New York harbor.

As of this writing the body of the Poglavnic remains in Madrid. The Ustache or any sympathy toward it is implicitly outlawed in Croatia,

Not Wanted

even to the extent of forbidding the displaying of the letter "U". Many Croatians, however, retain loyalty to the Ustache and its visions of Croatian nationalism, and hold secret ceremonies demonstrating such. Each year on the anniversary of the birthday of Ante Pavelic, a group of loyal followers of the founder of the Ustache gather in Zagreb, and in a ceremony blessed by a Catholic priest, swear eternal loyalty to the Ustache principles of Croatian nationalism, and swear hatred and vengeance to any and all Serbs and enemies of the Ustache. This they do over a crucifix, a dagger and a revolver.

Balkan memories are long!

We have seen in recent events what these people are capable of …

XIII.

BALKAN REVENGE?

What those people are capable of is biding their time over a period of years, to put together an intricate and elaborate plot wherein to inflict a most unique, cruel and vicious form of revenge on an enemy—"Balkan Revenge!"

One time when I was discussing this with my cousin, Juan Carlos, who is from Lima, Peru, and I started to mention this form of revenge, he cut in and said, "You kill the wife, the family…" Probably "they" have some knowledge of that sort of thing in South America. Which is—you do not kill your enemy, the object of your revenge. You kill his wife, his family, and leave him alive to suffer having had taken from him the most precious things in his life. To be tortured by memories, absence. What could be a more cruel and vicious form of exacting revenge?

To wit—for crimes, perhaps real and imagined, against the Croatian/Balkan people, perhaps including, probably including, the killing of one or more persons, a solemn oath of revenge would be sworn, no matter how long it might take.

A stream of "disinformation," to destroy a man's career, to gain power over him. To set him up for the ultimate revenge.

A Croatian/Balkan hit squad is assembled, moved into the United States. A plan is devised. The "victim" is gotten away from his house and drugged. The family is killed, without the victim's knowledge. He is spirited out of the country, under the subterfuge of "saving" him from the scandal that would destroy his career and quite possibly lead to a prison term, the destruction of his family relationship. To, say, Paraguay. Held prisoner in that country, he is bombarded with news media sources about the murder of his family, how he has been blamed for the killings and brutal disposal of the bodies, how he is a fugitive, and so on. More than any individual could take. Eventually he does go mad, and then is slipped into a lonely, unmarked grave somewhere on the vast pampa of Paraguay.

Is that what I think happened? I can only say that theory can not be disproven, any more than it can be proven. I would like to think that the Balkan revenge theory is what took place. If so, it would absolve William Bradford Bishop, Jr., of the horrific crime of brutally killing his entire family, if not of whatever crime(s) he might have committed against persons in the Balkans, back in the early 1960s and perhaps afterwards.

The Abyss of History is indeed deep. Far too often it does not surrender up the deepest secrets contained therein.

XIV.

DOCTOR AVIS
INTERVIEWS THE AUTHOR

Dr. A: I guess the first question has to be, "What do you think really happened, and why?"

DL: It boils down to one thing and one thing only—did William Bradford Bishop, Jr. kill his family or not? If he did not, then who did and why? The authorities from the very beginning focused on Bishop and no one else, because the circumstantial evidence seemed to be so over-whelming. But, there is a certain rush to judgment factor there. They never wanted to consider any alternative theories, or factors. It was not convenient. So, all along we have had Bishop as the one and only suspect.

I present an alternative theory that I think is rather intriguing and, in my mind, entirely possible. It cannot be proven, but then neither can it not be proven. I believe that the "Balkan Revenge" theory must be considered as a possible explanation, regardless of how far-fetched it might seem.

Dr. A: I rather like your "Balkan Revenge" theory. It appeals to my historical sense and my appreciation of the fanatical compulsion for revenge those people have. I do think that it is interesting to have a well constructed alternative theory in a case such as this. But, I must say that interesting as your theory is, I find it somewhat more than a bit far-fetched. But, since you have put it forward, let us run with it for a moment. I would have to ask about the time factor, the lapse of some dozen or so years between whatever Bishop might have done in Yugoslavia and the alleged enactment of "Balkan Revenge." Why so long?

DL: Admittedly, it is a rather long time, but those people had to investigate, identify, make all sorts of arrangements, wait for the exactly right time. All that takes years of planning. We have to assume that it did.

Dr. A: Why would the killers take the bodies to that remote spot in North Carolina, handle the bodies so crudely?

DL: They may have known about that spot from some previous activity. Or perhaps because of the proximity to the CIA facility across Albemarle Sound at Point Harvey. Also, by trundling the bodies miles from the house and making such a crude attempt to bury/burn them makes the crime all that more horrific, sadistic and unfeeling, the actions of a monster. We assume that is the impression they wanted shown in the media.

Dr. A: You focus, seemingly with good reason, on Croatia and Croatian fanatical nationalists. I have to ask what you think Bishop did on those incursions into Yugoslavia, what he was awarded a citation for bravery for?

DL: Well, I think it is obvious that he did something rather serious, perhaps killed somebody. And, rather peripherally, when I think about that it occurs to me that if he did kill someone he might have enjoyed it, enjoyed the thrill and power of it. In the service of his country, of course. I refer here to the "dark side" of Bishop that I perceived that senior year at Calhoun College at Yale—a side that no one else seems to have perceived, as far as I know. It is possible that over the years Bishop might have performed similar actions, in the service of his country of course. I do not mean to unnecessarily demean his reputation, but then how much worse can it get than being accused of and thought of having killed your entire family?

Dr. A: Why did Bishop show up in Jacksonville, North Carolina, making a $15.60 credit card purchase at a sporting goods store on the afternoon of the day when the bodies were "buried," seemingly unperturbed and wearing a suit? And who was the woman waiting outside holding a dog thought to be Bishop's on a leash? A woman the proprietor of that store remarked on as being part of "an item, they were definitely involved?" Something like that.

DL: I think his presence there in that unperturbed state can be explained by the possibility that he was not aware of what had happened, that the family had been killed. He thought he was being spirited out of the country to a new life. The woman was "a handler," part of the team, reassuring him, and so forth. Told him that there would be a boat trip. Maybe he thought he needed a pair of sneakers or something. She was watching and assisting him. The dog? Well, perhaps Bishop was unduly attached to the dog and asked if it could be brought along. Sure, they would have said, thinking it could always be tossed into the sea later.

Dr. A: So there you have Bishop in Jacksonville, North Carolina, thinking he is about to sail away into a new life with the assistance of his "Balkan protectors." Why should anyone believe that?

DL: They do not have to. It is just my theory which can be neither proven nor disproven. And which is, if I may say so, a pretty good alternative explanation for who killed the Bishop family.

Dr. A: We shall see. But for now, a few more questions about this Balkan theory. Getting back to the purchase of the hammer and the gas can, the filling of the can. How do you explain that?

DL; I would say that he was told to buy those items. If he questioned them he was told that the gas was needed for the vehicle, in case it ran low and they did not want to stop at a station. And the hammer? Needed to break locks of storage lockers where needed items were hidden, down in North Carolina where they would be headed to board a vessel. Regarding the vessel, one of the easiest ways to leave the United States undetected is by something like a fishing vessel, of which hundreds leave various ports and return unmonitored, especially in 1976.

Dr. A: Bishop leaves, or is taken, from Jacksonville, North Carolina. Why was the station wagon found four hundred miles away, on the west side of the Smoky Mountains?

DL: I think that was a diversion, to deflect attention away from Jacksonville. And also to create the illusion of a devious and dangerous fugitive. I think someone drove the car there, dragged items of Bishop's clothing around, and then left the car with various suspicious and possibly incriminating items.

Dr. A: You mean like the shotgun, the box of shells, and the jackets and suitcase full of men's clothing? How do you explain that?

DL: Nothing was ever said about Bishop owning a shotgun, so I am not sure where that came from and why it was in the car. Perhaps to further create the illusion of "armed and dangerous." The clothing, well, perhaps Bishop was told to take items like that when he drove to his "meeting" on the night of the killings. They were not needed where he was going, so the team just left them in the vehicle. Makes about as much sense as anything.

Dr. A: Yes, but all this is getting, as they say, "curiouser and curiouser." With all due pardon, of course. Did you say something about the team, if that is what it can be called, getting Bishop to South America, to Paraguay? How was that accomplished? And just what happened there?

DL: How they got him there is not important. Just that they did. And held him in confinement until over and over again he could be shown items from the media, incontestably authentic, that his family was dead, brutally murdered, the bodies taken to North Carolina and crudely partially buried and burned, and a nonchalant, uncaring Bishop shown before disappearing into the life of an international fugitive. More, probably, than the mind of any man could take. Perhaps his instability was helped along by drugs of some kind. He could easily be held in Paraguay, where there were many former Ustache and other Nazis. The benevolent regime of "El Benefactor," President General Alfredo Stroessner, could always be counted on the over-look various irregularities carried out by "friends."

Dr. A: Why Paraguay, and not Croatia, which you said that Annette Bishop's brother was quoted as saying that he "Seemed fond of that place?" And what do you think engendered Bishop's fondness for Croatia?

DL: Well, he certainly visited there at least once under positive conditions. And that would be the "tourist" trip he took with his wife after he got out of the army. It is possible that he had interacted positively with some group in Croatia, or Yugoslavia, other than Ustache or fanatical Croatian nationalists. Certainly something seems to have given him a fondness "for that place." Perhaps he thought his "rescuers" were going to take him to Croatia to start a new life. That might have had for him a certain amount of appeal.

Dr. A: So, according to your theory, Paraguay it was, torture and then a bullet to the back of the head or something, and an unmarked grave somewhere on the lonely pampa. End of story, right? But what about that wanted poster for Bishop in Spanish that I saw in Veracruz? And Detective Cady saying they thought he was in South America. That was, what, about twenty years after the murders and Bishop's disappearance. Explain that, please…

DL: Well, I think it entirely possible that when Bishop first arrived in Paraguay, or sometime not long after, someone saw him, heard about him, identified him as Bishop the wanted Gringo murderer. Perhaps notified some authorities, hoping for a reward, then thought better and backed away. Some authorities may have made some sort of investigation, but by that time Bishop was gone, underground— literally. Perhaps the file kicked around and information found its way north. And the notion that Bishop was in South America was in various files. And that would have been correct. He was in South America, dead and buried.

Dr. A: What about the mysterious letter, the one found in his file long after the crimes, from someone named Bangston, I believe, a former bank robber? That letter mentioned locales near where the bodies were found, and referred to some woman who might have been in a North Carolina prison, among other things. What comment do you have on that letter?

DL: That letter is rather hard to explain, particularly when there is reference to evidently five previous letters, none of which were found. Could

Bangston have been involved in some way with an ongoing investigation of Croatian nationalist activity in the United States? Possibly. Or just a loose screw of some kind. I really have no good, or even much of any, explanation for that letter, or previous ones. Just that perhaps Bishop was "up to something" that we will never know about.

Dr. A: Well, I guess that is the end of the story, if one goes with the "Balkan Revenge" theory. I admit that theory is intriguing and seems to sort of tie up the whole thing. And it can not be disproven. But, I have to say, with all due respect, that, as a professional historian, your theory is rather too far-fetched for me. I would say that it is possible but not likely. That, my friend, is my professional verdict, so to speak.

DL: Well, I am not surprised. In discussing the "Balkan Revenge" theory with a number of people I must say that they all seemed to lean toward your position. Perhaps it is just easier to accept the notion that Bishop killed his family for reasons we cannot know or understand.

Dr. A: Since that seems most likely, let us start at the beginning. Would that be the morning when he found out he was not getting a promotion, or some time earlier?

DL: I think we can agree that the failure to get the promotion, which he strongly felt he had earned and deserved, was a sort of spark that set him off. But, I would think that the tinder for this probably had been, shall we say, glowing for some time. Something in his professional life, private life. Some sort of tension, unease. We remember that he was being treated for "depression and alcoholism," conditions of which seemed mild and not readily discernible. But the causes might have been deep and destabilizing to his psyche.

Dr. A: So, the disappointment of that morning set him off, triggered some homicidal compulsion. I don't know what to call it, just some sort of psychotic break with reality. Could the purchase of the gas can and hammer, etc., have been pre-meditated or spur of the moment?

DL: That I cannot say, whether he had been contemplating these homicides, and the manner by which they were carried out. That seems rather brutal. Perhaps more acceptable would be the notion that he drifted into a psychotic break in his inner mind, while not connecting with his outward personality. That is getting a bit complex for me. But, for motive and behavior, I think there are perhaps two explanations. One, the first that I might consider, but perhaps the lesser of the two, might be that he had been ordered to resign from the State Department, perhaps to be revealed as some sort of spy, something shameful, and he never wanted his family to know whatever it was that he had done or been involved with. So, he killed them. In a psychotic break with reality.

Dr. A: Interesting. What about his subsequent behavior? And your other theory?

DL: As for subsequent behavior, we will get to that. My second theory involves a psychotic break with reality, but from a different source. Remember that no one has been able to come up with any sort of credible theory for the murders. Some cannot believe that he could have done such a thing, especially to the three beautiful boys whom he seemingly adored. But, my friend and classmate, the neurologist and psychiatrist tells me "that any one of us is capable of anything, anytime, anywhere, and anyhow." He has seen too much of that sort of thing. So, we have Bishop under some terrible and growing anxiety and tension, some of it directed toward his family, some directed elsewhere. Now, we remember that psychological theory introduced in chapter VI. I am going to present it here again, because it was too complex to easily remember:

"A theoretical psychological condition that might have applied to Bishop, and possibly explained his maniacal behavior, is something called 'Catathymic Crisis,' generally a term in forensic psychology. This theory was first presented by a Dr. Frederic Wertham in 1937 as a possible explanation for certain types of violent and seemingly motivation-less crimes. Dr. Wertham's theory describes a five stage process in which (1) a thinking disorder occurs within the mind of the criminal, (2) a plan is created to commit a violent criminal act, (3) internal emotional tension forces the commission of the criminal act, which leads to (4) a superficial calmness in which the need to commit the violent act is eliminated and normal activity can be conducted, and (5) the mind adjusts itself and understands that the thinking process that caused the commission of the criminal act was flawed and the mind makes adjustments in order to prevent any further criminal activity."

To put it a bit more simply, or in layman's terms, 'Catathymic Crisis' describes someone who kills a person or persons whom he is very close to and still grieves for the victims, as if he were completely innocent of any crime. Catathymic episodes start with anxiety and depression over emotionally tense relationships and end up with the belief that the only way out is murder.

It would seem that this theory might fit Bishop and explain his alleged behavior just a little too exactly. It is uncanny, and certainly resonates with the notions put forth in the Carolyn Banks novel *Darkroom*, which is based loosely on the Bishop case. Interestingly, my friend the neurologist and psychiatrist was not familiar with "Catathymic Crisis," It may be that the rapidly evolving field of psychology has discarded that theory and moved on to other things.

Rather imaginatively, in her novel Carolyn Banks postulates that her character William Holland (based of course on Bishop) was a victim of a CIA experiment with mind altering/control drugs, a program which in his case went wrong, horribly wrong, causing a psychotic break that resulted in the deaths of his family. The experiment was supposed to be entirely harmless, administered, monitored and observed by CIA psychiatrists. No long term or negative results were even remotely considered. The effects would quickly wear off and the subjects resume normal existence. Except in Bishop's case, at least as suggested by Banks in her novel, something went horribly wrong.

Dr. A: Interesting, perhaps remotely possible. Stuff like that did go on in the 1960s and 70s. It is remotely possible that Bishop could have been somehow involved with experiments in mind altering/controlled drug experiments. Perhaps even unwittingly. And, as you say, something went horribly wrong. Naturally, something like that would have to be covered up. Possible, but I have to say, I think perhaps somewhat farfetched. But, another theory that cannot be disproved.

DL: What we are confronted with here, however, is the apparent reality that the failure to get the promotion set Bishop off, and caused homicidal urges to move toward reality. He must have made the purchases that evening with some sort of plan in mind. Just under what psychological state we do not know.

We know he arrived home at approximately 6 p.m., and evidently spent his time in a normal manner, eating dinner, watching television, and so forth, while the family moved about him in their usual routines. We then can imagine that as 11 p.m. approaches his smoldering rage, or whatever it was, has reached a point where he can no longer contain it. He goes out to the station wagon, retrieves the hammer and comes back into the house and beats his wife to death as she sits in a chair reading. One or two powerful blows. And then upstairs to kill the three boys, forgetting that his mother is out walking the dog. He comes downstairs and confronts her as the enters. She runs up the stairs and locks herself in the bathroom. He batters down the door and bludgeons her to death. The entire family is dead.

Bishop is then in a completely psychotic state. It is possible that he thought the murders had been committed by another person. He decides to give the victims a loving and proper burial. Or perhaps just to get rid of them. The bodies are wrapped in blankets and loaded in the station wagon. He gets a suitcase, a few clothes, a couple of jackets (and a shotgun with a box of shells.) He does not know where he is going but it will be far away. He drives through the night to that spot just south of Columbia, North Carolina. Why that spot? Perhaps he had been familiar with it during some CIA training at the facility at Point Harvey on the other side of Albemarle Sound.

At that spot in the early morning he digs a small trench, places the bodies in it and sprinkles gasoline, and perhaps wipes the handles of the shovel and pitchfork. It is coming to him that something is wrong. He wants out of there. He tosses a match, gets in the vehicle and barrels away. Later that day he begins to feel calm, and cleans himself up, probably in a small motel. Does he put on a suit? Perhaps, but in looking through my files I can not find the reference to the suit. It is stuck in my mind from something I read, but it is possible that there was no suit. Whatever, he was clean, neatly dressed and calm and presentable. His mind began to clear of what had happened—as Carolyn Banks imagined.

Why Jacksonville? He may have known someone who lived there or near there—a "dark skinned woman." Who she was and what relationship she had with Bishop we do not know. She might have been a present or former "government employee." Bishop may have called her, seeking some sort of assistance. They meet on the afternoon of the day the bodies were discovered. She waits with the dog while he makes a small purchase in the sporting goods store. When they get in the station wagon she senses something is terribly wrong. It is the blankets, or perhaps Bishop's behavior, which might be disjointed and disturbed. Mumbling about something that happened, they had it coming, all sorts of things that frightened the woman. Bishop is evasive when she asks why he is in Jacksonville, where he is going.

The woman manages during a stop at a restaurant to call someone she knows with "a government agency," and explains about Bishop seemingly in a psychotic state and everything. The agency she calls immediately sends a team to intercept her and Bishop, and take Bishop into custody. He is not at that time a fugitive, for the bodies have not been identified and no police officers have entered the Bishop home. The team that takes Bishop into custody, drives to a remote location on the west side of the Smoky Mountains, where they have "facilities." When they get there they wait for some other "agents" who have psychological experience. They walk around a bit with Bishop on a trail and in the parking lot. It is gray and drizzly, and no one is around. Finally the other agents arrive and they take Bishop, and the station wagon, off to their facility to attempt to find out what is wrong with him. His may be a sensitive case, as alerted by the State Department. No one thinks to check on his family, not at that point. (They may have sent a team into the house surreptitiously, and determined more or less what probably happened.) They take the vehicle back to the parking lot and leave it as "abandoned" by Bishop. The interrogation continues, now focused on what happened to the family. The team is becoming very concerned. They want to know why he has "cracked up," what he thinks he has done, did do, when, where, with whom, and how. They want the works.

While this "interrogation" is going on word comes of the murders of Bishop's family, that he is the prime and only suspect and a fugitive. This is what they suspected, and it presents a problem, a major one. Input from higher sources is requested.

The situation is resolved roughly as follows: after reviewing the forensics of the murders and the evidence against Bishop, it is concluded that he has undoubtedly, in a psychotic break with reality, caused the deaths of his five family members. It is determined that he should not and can not be turned over to the authorities to be questioned, mentally evaluated and eventually placed on trial, because of (past) actions on behalf of the U.S. government. It is determined that he cannot be brought to trial, that would be inconvenient and very likely devastatingly embarrassing to "certain entities." So—NOT WANTED!

He would have to disappear without a trace. To be, as is said, "terminated with extreme prejudice." A team is brought in that deals with that sort of thing. A lethal injection—very "humane." A trip over to West Virginia to some government land that holds some old and very deep long abandoned coal mines. In Bishop goes, and probably Leo the dog with him, and on top of them several tons of rock.

Back at the spot in the west side of the Smoky Mountains the station wagon is discovered. Evidence suggests that Bishop had left it there, walked around a bit and then was "picked up by someone." This before he was known as a fugitive so the "someone" would not have been assisting a bloodthirsty murderer. Just a friend who might help Bishop to get over to Nashville or someplace, and then on out of the country. The myth of the fugitive had begun.

No asking of any awkward questions. The man is gone.

They are still looking for him. Officially, he is still WANTED.

Dr. A: That is quite an interesting progression of speculation. The most prominent question would be, if Bishop did kill his family, how did he get away and how does he live with himself?

DL: I would suggest that you read the Carolyn Banks novel, *Darkroom*, for an interpretation of that. I think she puts forth a pretty good postulation of how someone could live with that sort of "repressed memory." But, regardless of that, I have always had a very strong intuitive feeling that Bishop has not been alive for many years, not since shortly after the murders.

Dr. A: One last question, my friend. In something like this, a conspiracy, as you say, to silence Bishop and get rid of him so he could not be put on trial, involving agents and teams and so forth, eventually someone talks, do they not? Why not in this case? After all, it is not quite on the level of the Kennedy assassination. Maybe Bishop just did get away and has been a fugitive all this time, living with "repressed memory," or whatever you want to call it. Could you accept that?

DL: In this case, I suppose anything is possible where nothing can be proven nor disproven. One has to follow, to a large degree, one's intuition, wherever it leads. Sometimes into murky territory.

Dr. A: Well, I think you have produced a very interesting and challenging book here, and I tend to agree that early on "something happened" to Bishop. That sort of makes sense. Perhaps even "Balkan Revenge." But, I have to say that in the end it seems to me that all you have accomplished is to stir up and muddy the water. Considerably, I might say. Has that accomplished anything? Was that your purpose?

DL: I hope so. Perhaps that was my subliminal purpose. To get people thinking, asking questions. Maybe opening up new paths. I never expected to "solve" anything. There may be people out there who know a great deal more about all this than I do, but they are not talking. And it may be that someday something will turn up that will solve this case, or at least shed some new and valuable light. I would like to think so. People have been so accepting of the myth of Bishop as a worldwide fugitive. *America's Most Wanted. Unsolved Mysteries.* All that. Until now, I hope.

What are you thinking about, Doctor?

Dr. A: I am thinking about Brad at Yale, and that time in 1964 when we all had dinner in San Francisco. At Yale he always struck me as sort of positive and an all-American sort of guy. But since you mentioned a "dark inner side" I am wondering about that. And of how he said to me at dinner in San Francisco, "I wish I could be carefree like you guys here, but I can't." He never said why not.

XV.

GONE

His body will never be found. No one will ever really know what happened to him. That is, except for those who caused what happened to him. And where are they now?

That is the way when "things are taken care of…"

No one is naming any names here. None. Ever. Not of the one who has "disappeared." Nor of the ones who did "the taking care of…"

"Termination with extreme prejudice…"

That is the way of these things.

You don't want to know.

Or, do you?

Made in the USA
Lexington, KY
29 November 2010